BUT FOR THE GRACE OF GOD GO I

WHERE WOULD WE BE WITHOUT GRACE?

Incredible insights into the Grace of God
for survival and revival

Published by Terry J. Boyle
Copyright © Terry John Boyle 2024.

Unless otherwise noted, all scripture quotations are taken from the Holy Bible, New King James Version Copyright © 1979, 1980, 1982 by Thomas Nelson, Inc.

All rights reserved. No part of this book may be reproduced in any form, stored in a retrieval system, or transmitted in any form by any means—electronic, mechanical, photocopy, recording or otherwise—without the prior written permission of the publisher, except as provided by Australian copyright law.

Words in capitals, or in bold or italics are the emphases of the author Terry Boyle – terryjohnboyle@bigpond.com

Cover & typeset by Carl Butel at Deep Image – carl@deepimage.net.au

Cataloguing-in-Publication data is available from the National Library of Australia.

ISBN 978-0-646-89252-8
eBook ISBN 978-0-646-89253-5

Acknowledgments

I thank my wife, Caroline, for her incredible love and support over the years while in ministry and patience while writing books. I also thank our children Amanda, Felicity, Andrew, and Sharon for their love and support.

Thank you to our daughter Amanda for her wisdom and input and especially to Carl Butel, her husband, for his fantastic cover design and internal layout and for getting the book ready for the publisher.

To my son Andrew, a Baptist minister, for his scrutiny, wise suggestions, inspiration, and endorsement of the book.

I thank John Latta for taking the time to read the manuscript, make valuable comments, and write an endorsement.

Thank you to Life Ministry Church in Melbourne, where I began my full-time ministry with the late Hal Oxley and the team in Melbourne.

Thanks to the late John Pasterkamp and those in Papua New Guinea, where we ministered for some years nationwide and established a Bible College.

Thank you to all those at Centre Church in Lismore, where we ministered for 21 years as the senior pastor and chairman of Summerland Christian College.

To our association with A2A over many years and the many church leaders who have impacted our lives.

BUT
FOR THE
GRACE
OF GOD
GO I

CONTENTS

Endorsements

Introduction

Quotable Quotes on Grace

A definition of the Grace of God

1. Where would we be without Grace?
2. Jesus came full of Grace and Truth
3. Like a puppet on a string
4. Waltzing to the tune of Grace
5. The last remnants of religion
6. Hallmarks of Grace in a Church
7. Grace to forgive
8. Parables of Grace and Truth
9. His Grace is sufficient
10. The manifold Grace Gifts of God
11. Who has bewitched you?
12. Grace in the Book of Acts
13. Grace and the work of the Holy Spirit
14. The Throne of Grace, not judgment
15. Shouts of Grace Grace
16. A Safety Net of Grace
17. Future Grace
18. Portals of Grace

Endorsement

I have studied and taught on the grace of God for over 35 years. This book by Terry addresses so many essential truths we desperately need to understand.

One is the issue of guilt and shame and how the grace of God also frees us from religious shame. We live in a performance culture that can affect how we think about God. People feel that we need to appease the triune God through our behaviour. It will not erase our shame. Our problem is not a behavioural fight but an identity issue. The finished work of Jesus removed the shame (defective mindset), and we are now "born from above" in Christ with a new identity. We are a new creation completely forgiven.

Terry points out that our discipleship, service, obedience, morality, and worship are all critical spiritual disciplines that can all be turned into performance-based Christianity if we do not understand the grace of God. We can fall into a performance trap that distorts our understanding of God and what He has done for us. This book by Terry, "But for the grace of God go I," is so important for us if we are to gain a greater appreciation of the character and nature of God.

Grace gives us rest, not laziness. Biblical rest means vocation. So, we are not working but fulfilling our calling with great joy as Christians. Terry shares how grace-based churches will be activated to serve their community, especially the disadvantaged, because grace works in us to will and do His good pleasure.

In Ephesians 2, Paul writes words that speak directly against performance-based Christianity.

"It is by grace you have been saved, through faith, and this is not from yourselves, it is the gift of God not by works so that no one can boast." Ephesians 2:8-9.

This book unfolds a much greater understanding and insight into following Christ in today's world. We need to know that Grace is the power of God to live a godly life.

Clear teaching on grace is a rare commodity. So I highly recommend this book and pray it will be read and lived.

John Latta

Senior Minister of "Living Grace Church" (Church of Christ)
Tweed Heads, N.S.W., Australia.

Endorsement

I was thrilled that my father decided to act on my suggestion (or temptation, as he put it) to write a book on grace. Looking back at my teen years, I recall that Dad was captivated by the subject of grace.

To him, grace was not just a theological doctrine but something real and tangible, an ever unfolding revelation, and a gift that quite literally keeps on giving.

Dad has always been a captivating storyteller, and the personal stories he shares help bring the subject of grace to life in an engaging and memorable way. I also found the insights and applications of grace beneficial, especially the need for grace and truth to work together.

Like all of Dad's books, this book flows out of a lifetime of devotion to Jesus and His teachings. I am sure this book will challenge, bless, and encourage you.

Andrew Boyle M.Div.

Associate Pastor of Fairfield Christian Family Church
Brisbane, Australia.

BUT FOR THE GRACE OF GOD GO I

Introduction

This book is my fourth, and with each one, a trigger point has inspired me to write.

With my first book, **Unlocking Your Purpose**, I had an unfinished manuscript that I had almost given up on. After speaking at a church, someone who knew nothing about me writing a book came up and said, "I feel I have a word for you." They had put it on their phone, and when they showed me, it read, "Finish the Book," so I did.

With my second book, **Enjoying your twilight years**. After looking through an old photo album and glancing in the mirror, I realised I was in my twilight years. But despite the apparent aging process we all face, I was still rejoicing and wanted to share some keys to enjoying our twilight years with others.

In my third book, **Hungry for God**, I commented in my second book about how I had fasted and prayed for 40 days while God was pouring out His Spirit on the mission field in PNG. I had kept a journal and said, "I could probably write another book on extracts from that experience." After looking into it and going through my journal, I decided to. So I Did.

I talked with my son about my third book and said, *"Andrew, that is my last book,"* he replied, *"What about the Grace of God? You have a great understanding and revelation of the grace of God."* I said, *"Andrew, don't tempt me."* As you can see, this is one temptation I gave in to. I have already started on my fifth book, titled **The Ambiguous Kingdom,** which I also blame Andrew for.

But I thought to myself, how do you write another book on the grace of God? So I questioned the Lord, *"Surely, there are enough books already on grace?"* I felt He replied, *"There can never be enough grace."*

I love the phrase *"But for the GRACE of God Go I,"* hence the book title. Some say this goes back to Francis of Assisi. This lacks historicity. However, there is evidence that John Bradford spoke these words in the sixteenth century. I will elaborate on this in the first chapter.

I hope this book will be as enlightening and a source of encouragement for you as it has been for me in writing it. I believe there are keys in it that will help you survive and revive.

Quotable Quotes on Grace

"Grace saves us from a life without God – even more, it empowers us for a life with God." – Richard Foster (front cover)

"Grace is the voice that calls us to change and then gives us the power to pull it off." – Max Lucado

"Certainly, we should be very active in seeking God, and Jesus Himself called us to 'ask, seek, knock' in order to find Him, yet those who enter a relationship with God inevitably look back and recognise that God's grace had sought them out, breaking them open to new realities." – Tim Keller

"Grace comes into the soul, as the morning sun into the world; first a dawning; then a light; and at last the sun in his full and excellent brightness." – Thomas Adams

"Grace is a system of living whereby God blesses us because we are in Jesus Christ, and for no other reason at all." – Steve McVey

A Definition of the Grace of God

"It is understood by Western Christians to be a spontaneous gift from God to people" – *"generous, free and totally unexpected and undeserved"* – *"that takes the form of divine favour, love, clemency, and a share in the divine life of God."*

– Wikipedia

Chapter 1

Where would we be without Grace?

I mentioned in my introduction that the title is an old saying that some say goes back to Francis of Assisi, a Catholic Friar who founded the Franciscan order. The context and historicity of this saying attributed to him is uncertain.

However, there is plenty of evidence that the English reformer John Bradford said these words when he was a prisoner in the Tower of London for alleged crimes against Queen Mary the First.

When John Bradford saw prisoners led to their execution, he exclaimed, "But for the Grace of God go I." By saying this, John implies that by God's grace, he is fortunate that he's not one of them, and if it weren't for the grace of God extended to him, he would be.

Where would you be?

Perhaps we could all apply this saying to ourselves as we look back at our old life before we became Christians. Where would we be without the grace of God? I hate to think where I would be. What about you?

Without grace, we would be in a lot of trouble. Jesus tells us that the flesh is weak and vulnerable to temptation and sin. The apostle Paul was well aware of the problem.

"For I know that in me (that is, in my flesh) nothing good dwells; for to will is present with me, but how to perform what is good I do not find. For the good that I will to do, I do not do; but the evil I will not to do, that I practice. Now, if I do what I will not to do, it is no longer I who do it, but sin that dwells in me." Romans 7:18-20.

Does this sound familiar? It is a problem we all wrestle with. However, in this context, Paul explains that trying to keep the law religiously is not the answer. He tells us that Christ is the only answer.

Welcome to the grace of God

Thank God for His grace. No one would qualify to inherit the Kingdom of God if it were not for the grace of God.

"Do you not know that the unrighteous shall not inherit the kingdom of God" 1 Corinthians 6:9.

No one would inherit the kingdom of God if it were not

for the grace of God. We would all be deemed unrighteous, lost, and needing a Saviour.

Paul goes on to say, *"Do not be deceived. Neither fornicators, nor idolaters, nor adulterers, nor homosexuals, nor sodomites, nor thieves, nor covetous, nor drunkards, nor revilers, nor extortioners will inherit the kingdom of God."* Verses 9-10.

This extensive list disqualifies many people from inheriting the kingdom of God. If we are honest, some of us probably identify with one or more.

Thank God for His grace because Paul says, *"And such were some of you. But you were washed, but you were sanctified, but you were justified in the name of the Lord Jesus Christ and by the Spirit of our God."* Verse 11.

And such WERE some of you! Note the past tense. By the grace of God, our past is behind us. Instead of going to a lost eternity, we were saved by grace and on our way to heaven because of Christ.

We can do nothing to justify ourselves or make ourselves right with God; Christ has done it for us through the cross. It is God's grace extended to us while we were still sinners.

The side effects of sin

Now that I am in my twilight years, I am on medication for

a few ailments. All these come with warnings of possible side effects. Sin also has side effects that can sometimes linger on for years after becoming a Christian.

The most prominent of these seems to be guilt and shame, which usually remind us of our past sins and mistakes. These thoughts that flare up from time to time make us feel terrible, and they hinder our faith. I have done things I have been ashamed of and have had some battles with lingering feelings of guilt and shame.

In her book 'Released from Shame' Dr. Sandra Wilson states, "Shame is different from Guilt." "Guilt tells me I made a mistake." "Shame shouts that I AM a mistake."

Because of this, some people may need counseling and prayer to work through these issues even though technically, from a theological point of view, they have been dealt with at the cross.

For those who struggle in this area, Dr. Allan Meyer and his wife Helen have designed an excellent programme to help people through difficulties they have experienced in life. It is called "Careforce Lifekeys," which I recommend for every church.

The power of the blood

By the grace of God, the past is behind us, but the devil reminds us of our guilt and shame. There is no greater power than the Blood of the Lamb to enable us to overcome past accusations and walk in victory.

"The accuser of our brethren, who accused them before our God day and night, has been cast down. And they overcame him by the blood of the Lamb and the word of their testimony, and they did not love their lives to the death." Revelation 12:11-12.

The devil has no answer to the blood of Christ.

One night, I had a phone call from a desperate young girl. She was involved in the occult and living with her grandmother, who was into witchcraft and the leader of a coven. She felt she needed deliverance but was scared to leave the coven.

She was ringing from a public phone box. I said I think I can help you if you come and see me. Then I said let me pray for you now. I prayed for her, and as soon as I mentioned the blood of Christ, There was a muffled noise, and the phone went dead. So, after a while, I hung up. Surprisingly, she was sitting on the doorstep when I arrived at my office the next day. After more prayer and deliverance, by God's grace, she became a Christian by putting her faith in Christ as her Saviour and Lord.

A few days later, we went to help her leave her grandmother's house. She collected her stuff, and the grandmother cast spells on her as she departed. But I said, "They will all fall to the ground just like the blood of Jesus;" As soon as she heard that, the grandmother ran back into the house.

Although we know we are forgiven and justified through faith in Christ, the devil has ways of reminding us of our past sins that make us feel unworthy to serve the Lord.

But the devil hates the blood. The reformer Martin Luther discovered that doing penance was futile. He had a revelation that it was by faith in the finished work of Christ that he was justified. One night, the devil woke him up and presented him with a list of past sins to accuse him and make him feel unworthy. But apparently, he looked at the devil and the list of sins and said, *"Now write across the list that the blood of Christ has cleansed me from all sin."* (1John1:7). Then Luther rolled over and went back to sleep.

Do not let the devil accuse or condemn you. *"There is, therefore, no condemnation to those who are in Christ Jesus, who do not walk according to the flesh, but according to the Spirit. For the law of the spirit of life in Christ Jesus has set me free from the law of sin and death."* Romans 8:1-2.

If you are in Christ, then you are free from condemnation. No law, devil, demon, or person can condemn you because of the blood of Christ and your faith in the finished work of the cross.

The riches of His grace

Why does the apostle Paul constantly write about the grace of God? It is not only because he experienced the grace of God extended to him but also because of the revelation he had of the riches of His grace.

"In Him, we have redemption through His blood, the forgiveness of sins, according to the riches of His grace." Ephesians 1:7

The Apostle points out that this redemption we have through His blood and the forgiveness of sins is all because of the riches of His grace. Only the blood of Jesus could remove the stain of sin.

We live in the church age, the age of grace. But the scripture indicates that God will continue to display the riches of His grace and mercy throughout the generations to come, even to eternity.

"That in the ages to come, He might show the exceeding riches of His grace in His kindness toward us in Christ Jesus. For by grace, you have been saved through faith, and that not of yourselves; it is the gift of God, not of works lest anyone should boast." Ephesians 2:7-9.

Our self-righteous works will not save us; it is the grace of God and our faith in Christ that we obtain eternal life and a place in heaven.

Three main areas of the riches of His grace –

Many scholars shuffle grace into three main areas that affect our lives and our relationship with God. (although I suspect there are more).

1. **Prevenient grace** – This is grace that comes before our conversion; it calls us into a relationship with God, even before we are aware of God. It prepares us for an encounter with God.

2. **Justifying grace** – This is when Christians and non-Christians abandon all those vain attempts to justify themselves through religious and moral practices and accept that they are justified by faith in Christ alone.

3. **Sanctifying grace** - This enables us to grow into the image of Christ and leads us to inner and outer sanctification and holiness that is worthy of our calling.

We will be looking at all these aspects and more as we unfold the pages of this book together.

Has Christ died in vain?

Paul was forever mindful of the power of the cross concerning trying to justify ourselves by keeping the law. To do so would be to set aside the grace of God, and Christ would have died in vain.

"I have been crucified with Christ; it is no longer I who live, but Christ lives in me; and the life that I now live in the flesh I live by faith in the Son of God, who loved me and gave Himself for me. "I do not set aside the grace of God; for if righteousness comes through the law, then Christ died in vain." Galatians 2:20-21.

Paul points to the cross and states that this is what the grace of God is all about. I can do nothing to make myself any more righteous than I am because of Christ. If I try, I frustrate God's grace.

When we ignore the work of the cross, we revert to faith plus works to make ourselves more righteous and justify ourselves by our works rather than the work already accomplished for our righteousness at Calvary.

Paul says he now lives by faith in the Son of God. It enables him to walk in victory and live as a Christian. He says, "He loved me and gave Himself for me." He has done the same for you and me. Thank you, Lord!

Do not dwell on the past

Paul never let the past hold him back from ministry and becoming an apostle. He must have felt guilt and shame because of his history. Before becoming a Christian, he persecuted the church.

"For I am the least of the apostles. Who am not worthy to be called an apostle because I persecuted the church of God. But by the grace of God, I am what I am, and His grace towards me was not in vain; but I laboured more abundantly than they all, yet not I but the grace of God which was with me." 1 Corinthians 15:9-10.

Three times in these verses, Paul refers to the grace of God that has enabled him to overcome the guilt and shame of the past and to enter the ministry and serve Christ as an Apostle. In the back of his mind, he knows he is not worthy of that title and that it is only by the grace of God that he functions in that role.

It applies to all of us as Christians, especially those in

ministry. We are all what we are, in whatever capacity we serve Christ by the grace of God.

Chapter 2

Jesus came full of Grace and Truth

Unlike the law of Moses, Jesus came to us full of grace and truth. This is at the heart of Christianity.

Some years ago, I was preaching on love and marriage in Papua New Guinea and burst into a verse of that old song, "Love and marriage go together like a horse and carriage; you can't have one without the other."

It must have sounded pretty good because someone approached me later and wanted to know when I would teach that new chorus.

The point is that grace and truth go together. You should not have one without the other. We could never meet God's standard of truth contained in the law without grace. We would become judgemental and frustrated because we could never keep all the requirements of the law.

But on the other hand, can you imagine grace without truth? There would be no guidelines to follow, and we would end up in anarchy, looking for purpose and direction. We need both truth and grace as Christians to live a victorious life.

Some Christians still gravitate to one side or the other, either truth or grace. They rarely exhibit a healthy Christ-like fulness of grace and truth.

The Word became flesh

"And the Word became flesh and dwelt among us, and we beheld His glory, as of the only begotten of the Father, full of grace and truth." John 1:14.

He could have approached us as a judge because we failed to keep the law of Moses. But He did not come to judge and condemn us but to save us from our sins. So, to do this, He needed to come to us full of grace and truth.

It is worth noting, leading up to verse 14, how John is probably aiming at reaching the Jews with this message. The Jews upheld the book of Genesis as the word of God. They knew how Genesis started with the scripture -

"In the beginning, God created the heavens and the earth" Genesis 1:1.

So, John starts his gospel with "In the beginning" to get their attention, then adds more information about this God who was in the beginning. He calls Him the Word. Then, he explains who the Word was!

"In the beginning was the Word, and the Word was with God, and the Word was God. He was in the beginning with God. All things were made through Him, and without Him, nothing was made that was made.".... *"And the Word became flesh and dwelt among us."...* *"Full of grace and truth."* John 1:1-3 and 14.

John states that the Word was Jesus. He was the creator of heaven and earth in the beginning. So, John says that the God the Jews worshipped has now come in the flesh as Jesus and implies that Jesus is the Messiah they have been waiting for.

From a Christian perspective, He came to us full of grace and truth to enable us to live a life of freedom from the condemnation of the law that came through Moses.

How does this affect us?

It has a profound effect on Christianity. Grace and truth blend through the gospel's message, making Christianity unique compared to different religions. In all other religions, grace and truth never seem to meet. They either dispense justice at the expense of grace or grace at the expense of justice.

Jesus coming to us full of grace and truth is unique to Christianity. If we major in grace alone, we end up with a wishy-washy sentimental approach to the gospel. If we focus on the truth alone, we end up with a cold-hearted, legalistic, judgemental approach to the gospel.

In his book *"The Grace and Truth Paradox,"* Randy Alcorn writes, "Truth without grace brings self-righteous legalism, poisons the church, and pushes the world away from Christ. Grace without truth breeds moral indifference and keeps people from seeing their need for Christ."

Jesus mastered the art of accepting everyone without accepting everything they did. We face the same challenge today.

God is not indifferent

God is not indifferent to sin and the way we live. He did not create us in His image and then lose interest in us. God loves us and has given us His word for our well-being and benefit. We have the freedom of choice, but God guides us with His word so we can choose what is best for us.

To some extent, our culture is inclined to exclude God by seeing that the human condition is basically good (except for occasional despots). So, the world is out to improve its good condition without needing help from God.

It opens the door to ungodliness. God sees that our major problem is still sin and its detrimental effect on our culture and future.

The world is inclined to accept grace on its terms – but hates the truth that exposes sin. (John 3:19-21). It means the world wants the church to embrace sinners and sometimes the sin itself by grace. The problem is that we live in an age where just about everything is to be tolerated.

I had someone say to me, "I do not think God is all that

interested in what we do with our genitals." They were referring to our sexuality and our lifestyle. I can understand people saying that these days, but we would have to disagree if we examined the scriptures.

Some Christians would argue that if you love someone, you would accept everything about them. I love my wife and everything about her. But when we do not agree on some things, does that mean I stop loving her? Of course not! I can love and accept someone just as they are, but I do not have to agree with everything they say and do.

Controversial issues

When it comes to controversial issues, there is much debate on how grace and truth can flow together to resolve some of the complex problems we face today.

For example, one current issue is debatable and divisive in the church today. It is the issue of "same-sex marriage." It becomes complicated because of its social acceptance and the legal ramifications for those who may oppose it. Grace demands that we try to reach people with the gospel. God loves everyone and sent His son to die for all humanity, including same-sex partners. All of us are sinners who need to be saved by grace. But we are also required to uphold the truth.

I can understand the dilemma for Christians who face having sons, daughters, or friends who have chosen this lifestyle. What should they do? They should never stop loving them, but it does not mean they must condone their lifestyle.

The sanctity of marriage

When it comes to marriage, the world would have the church compromise truth and turn it into an unholy sacrament - that of same-sex marriage, which violates the sanctity of marriage ordained by God in the beginning. Fornicators and adulterers also violate the sanctity of marriage.

"Marriage is honourable among all, and the bed undefiled; But fornicators and adulterers God will judge." Hebrews 13:4.

God ordained it this way in the beginning. It was the foundation for humanity to live by. "God created them male and female" Genesis 1:27. He created Adam and Eve, not Adam and Steve, to multiply, be fruitful, and replenish the earth. God ordains no other pattern for the human race. Therefore, call it what you like, but such a union cannot be a valid biblical marriage in the eyes of God.

It is an area many church leaders and churches are facing today. They have to make choices. Will they marry or not marry practicing same-sex couples? If they do, to what extent will they involve them in the life of the church? Sure, we all need the gospel of grace. Remember, I quoted earlier from Corinthians.

"And so were some of you."

The title of this book, *"But for the Grace of God Go I,"* implies that if it wasn't for God's grace, we might end up going the same way. So where would we be without the grace of God?

However, this scripture states, "And so WERE some of you," this intimates that they had repented and were saved by grace and in fellowship because they had turned away from their sin and turned to God for forgiveness and salvation. The early church showed grace but did not compromise the truth.

It is a touchy subject, and we need the wisdom of God as to how we approach and apply it.

Where are you pitching your tent?

Interestingly, when Abraham and his nephew Lot parted company, Lot *"Pitched his tent toward Sodom."* Genesis 13:12 (NLT).

It ended up being an unwise decision. Lot may not have known how God felt about the city. God was angry with Sodom and Gomorrah because the people were evil and wicked in His sight. So He planned to destroy Sodom and Gomorrah.

When Abraham heard that God was about to destroy the city, he said, *"Would you destroy the righteous with the wicked?"* Genesis 18:23.

Then Abraham began to plead, intercede, pray, and ask God to spare the city for the sake of fifty righteous, to which God agreed. But it became evident that God could not find fifty. Abraham kept pleading with God until he got down to ten, and then Abraham gave up. It gives us an understanding of how corrupt the city had become.

But Lot was instructed to leave the city and flee to safety and was told not to look back. The grace of God saved him. However, Lot lost his wife in the process; she looked back and became a pillar of salt.

So, if we use this story as an analogy, we should consider which direction we are pitching our tent today.

Grace teaches us sanctification

Grace is not a license to get away with practicing evil. It is not giving us the go-ahead to sin. Paul asks, *"Shall we continue in sin that grace may abound? Certainly not!"* Romans 6:1.

Grace teaches us to live a godly life. *"For the grace of God that brings salvation has appeared to all men, teaching us that, denying ungodliness and worldly lusts, we should live soberly, righteously, and godly in the present age, looking for the blessed hope and glorious appearing of our great God and Saviour Jesus Christ."* Titus 2:11-13.

Without getting into Old Testament scriptures, other New Testament references state how God feels about this lifestyle. Our sympathetic feelings and emotions should not override the word of God. The truth of the word is evident in Romans 1:26-32, 1 Corinthians 6:9-11, and 1 Timothy 1:9-11.

The Bible teaches us to establish moral boundaries based on God's word. These are not only for our well-being but also to preserve humanity from destroying itself through disease and corruption. Jesus said the flesh is weak, implying it is vulnerable to temptations. It is only by the grace of God that we overcome and survive.

I love the message of grace. But I do not want to compromise the truth of God's word. So we are to uphold the truth but simultaneously hope and pray that all would respond to the gospel of grace, come to a place of repentance, and receive Christ as their Lord and Saviour.

Jesus came as the Messiah, full of grace and truth; He superseded the law. Jesus challenges the legalistic stand that the Scribes and Pharisees take on upholding the law of Moses.

Jesus displays grace and truth

Jesus displays grace and truth to the woman they brought to Him who was taken in the act of adultery. Her accusers said to Jesus -

"Moses in the law commanded us that such should be stoned. But what do you say?.... He said to them he who is without sin among you, let him cast the first stone." John 8:5-7.

When they became convicted by their conscience, they, one by one, from the eldest, dropped their stones and walked away.

Jesus said to the woman, *"Where are those accusers of yours? Has no one condemned you?"* She said, *"No one Lord."* And Jesus said to her, *"Neither do I condemn you, go and sin no more."* Verses 9-11.

Grace does not condemn her like the law. But Jesus said to the woman, "Go and sin no more." It implies that she is now responsible for abiding by the word. I wonder if she was able to do that. Did she fail again? Or was she successful? I know for most of us, it is often a struggle. But Grace allows us to repent of our sins and put things right with God.

We could never keep the law with all its rules and regulations. God gave it to be our schoolmaster to lead us to Christ and to show us how dependent we are on grace and faith in Christ for our justification.

"But before faith came, we were kept under guard by the law, kept for the faith that would afterward be revealed. Therefore, the law was our tutor (School Master) to bring us to Christ so that we might be justified by faith. But after faith has come, we are no longer under a tutor." Galatians 3:23-25.

May God give us the wisdom to enjoy this newfound freedom in Christ.

Although some would say grace alone would be a lot more fun, we could get away with heaps, but it would only give us a license to sin, leading to utter confusion, chaos, and eventual destruction without truth. Thank you, Jesus, for coming to us full of grace and truth.

Chapter 3

Like a puppet on a string

By the grace of God, I was born again in a little church plant that met in a house in my hometown in Horsham, Victoria, Australia.

I will never forget how I felt when I first became a Christian. I had committed my life to Christ. I was overwhelmed with joy. I felt so free. Jesus had forgiven me. I knew I had eternal life and was going to heaven no matter what happened.

What a relief. I had been searching for God for years and did not know how to find Him. But He found me.

As a teenager, we had a tradition in our family when we had roast chicken; whoever got the wishbone would make a wish. I would begin making a list of things I would love to have, but always, at the end of the list, I wished I knew God. He must have heard the cry of my heart.

Early days as a Christian

As a new Christian, I was hungry for God and would devour books and tapes in those days and feed on as much of God's word as possible.

I attended church regularly and felt God was preparing me for ministry. While all this was happening, I met Caroline, who became my lovely wife. After we were married, we enrolled in a Bible College in Adelaide and spent two years in College. Our prominent lecturers were Barry Chant and Leo Harris. They were great days of learning and training for the ministry. After graduating, we moved to Melbourne to enable my wife to finish off a few subjects to complete her degree in Agricultural Science.

Hal Oxley, the senior pastor of the church we attended in Melbourne, encouraged us to pioneer a church in Healesville, a small drive from the Eastern Suburbs of Melbourne, where we lived. We were still both working in secular jobs. It was hard work, driving to hold meetings every weekend, but after a year, up to forty people attended on a Sunday morning.

Then came a massive change for us. Hal invited me to join the ministry team in Melbourne full-time. I handed the church in Healesville to another young pastor and accepted the invitation.

Initially, it was a wonderful experience for me. I was on a steep learning curve; it was an exciting time. God was pouring out His Spirit; many turned to Christ, and some were healed and delivered. Yet I felt something was missing. I could not put my finger on it then, but I was under continual pressure to meet certain expectations. After a few years, I began feeling like a puppet on a string.

Trying hard to measure up

Hal was a colonel in the army and a successful businessman before entering the ministry. He was a strict disciplinarian. The church seemed like a military institution. I was always trying hard to measure up. I admit the discipline was good for me, and I was thankful for it, but I sometimes felt he was way out of touch with reality in some of his expectations.

I remember Hal making a comment that stunned me. He said, "Any pastor with time for golf can't be on the front line." I loved golf and still do. It is my source of relaxation (sometimes frustration). But while I was in Melbourne, I stopped playing golf. Hal set the bar too high; the higher he set it, the higher you had to jump. It left me feeling that I was not good enough and maybe didn't belong in the ministry.

Too many rigid rules and high standards led to continual pressure to perform. I felt trapped and lacked freedom in the Spirit.

I will share with you what may seem trivial examples now, but they bothered me at the time and robbed me of the joy of the Lord.

I was to open the meeting in prayer one night, and Hal said, "Terry, get up there on the platform and give a rip-roaring CLC opening prayer." I did my best but thought at the time, why does prayer need to be a performance? It should be from the heart, and what happened to the leading of the Holy Spirit? I may have required some guidance, but I did not want to continue to feel like a puppet on a string performing for an audience.

At the first wedding I officiated at, Hal was in attendance, and I glanced up and saw him write something in his little black book. My negative mindset told me I was in trouble. Sure enough, he later called me into his office and said that he noticed at the wedding that the creases in my trousers needed pressing. Maybe I needed to hear that, but I wanted more than criticism. I desired an encouraging word. It was my first ever wedding.

There was another time when I was to preach, and we were in a side room about to come on to the platform, and Hal got stuck into me to get on to the cleaners as they had missed cobwebs on the ceiling in the room we were in.

At the next minister's meeting, I took a risk and told him I did not think it was the right time to talk about cobwebs before I was to preach. He did not say anything then, but years later, he apologised, thanked me, and told me I was right to speak up and challenge him.

I mean no disrespect

I mean no disrespect to Hal. I grew to love and admire him. He was a great teacher and an exceptional leader. It was a different era that focused on doing things a certain way. Hal mellowed over the years, and we would meet up with Hal and

Jill nearly every year when they holidayed on the Gold Coast.

I do not want to be nit-picking. I know these incidents sound like minor misdemeanors, but when you start in ministry, they mount up, rob you of your joy, and make you feel miserable. These little things get to you, and you become discouraged when you are trying so hard to please everyone. Especially when the only feedback you seem to get is negative.

Our ministry team members were reprimanded at the next weekly administrative meeting whenever we failed to meet specific standards. But we were hardly ever encouraged for what we had done well.

Is God mad at me?

As a church, we arranged an itinerary for Johny Ortiz, a brilliant speaker who had experienced a revival in his church in South America.

I had the privilege of driving him to a country town for a meeting about two and a half hours from Melbourne. During the service, they took up a love offering for Johny; thinking I was doing the right thing, I gave it to him. When we eventually returned to Melbourne, Hal asked me for the love offering. When I told him I had already given it to Johny, he got mad at me and said we had to take our expenses out of it.

Even though I protested my innocence, I thought God must also be mad at me for making such a foolish mistake.

After a while, you wonder what God thinks of your performance. Is He mad at you, or does His grace and love override your mistakes?

During my six years in Melbourne, I felt my ministry was a dichotomy; It was both exciting and frustrating at the same time. Something was missing. I was not enjoying complete freedom in Christ. I knew in my heart that God was *"Compassionate and gracious, slow to anger and abounding in loving-kindness."* Psalm 103:8. I was not feeling the grace or the love. I was more like a puppet on a religious string.

Beyond an Angry God

I went through a stage where I questioned what God was like. Was He waiting for me to step out of line so He could get angry with me and withdraw His blessing?

Here is an extract from an ad promoting the book "Beyond an Angry God" by Steve McVey: "Have you ever felt as if God were mad at you? When things go wrong, do you ever wonder if He is punishing you?" Steve reveals where toxic thoughts like this come from – "A twisted view of an angry God that permeates the Western culture and church."

I had the privilege of hearing Steve McVey preach when John Latta had Steve in his church at Mount Tambourine. His revelation of grace was incredible. What he had to say astounded me.

John and his wife Jill now lead the Church of Christ at "Living Grace" Tweed Heads on the border of the Gold

Coast. John also brings a great word on understanding and applying the grace of God to our lives.

When religion overrules grace, we look in the mirror, and what do we see? It reflects our failures rather than what the word says about who we are in Christ. We are all under pressure to conform to specific religious standards set by man rather than the word of God.

The perfectionist trap

Religion and legalism demand that we strive for perfection. Christians and non-Christians can fall into the perfectionist trap. Thomas Curran, associate professor at the London School of Economics, describes himself as a "recovering perfectionist." In his book "The Perfectionist Trap," he says, "A lot of my perfectionism comes from worrying about not being good enough or that I don't belong."

He describes three types of perfectionism emerging today;

(a) **Self-orientated** – An inner pressure to be perfect that manifests as a sense of never being good enough.

(b) **Other-orientated** – Expecting others to be perfect and calling them out when they fall short.

(c) **Socially prescribed** – The feeling that others expect perfection and constantly judge your performance.

He goes into some detail as to how to overcome this problem but sums it up by suggesting we come to grips with accepting that "good enough is good enough." I remember my dad was invited to become an elder in the Uniting Church but refused because he felt he was not good enough.

When asked how he handled criticism for some movie roles, Anthony Hopkins replied, "My philosophy is that what people say about me is none of my business. I am who I am and do what I do. I expect nothing and accept everything. And that makes life easier. We live in a world where funerals are more important than the deceased. Marriage is more important than love. Looks are more important than the soul. We live in a packaging culture that despises content." –Anthony Hopkins.

In other words, we live in a world that focuses on our image and performance instead of actual content. No matter who we are, our nationality, or our status in life, we are acceptable and lovable in Christ because of His forgiveness and redemption through His blood on the cross. We do not have to fall into a perfectionist trap. We have been set free by the grace of God.

Avoid the religious rut

Sometimes, the Western Church seems to get into a religious rut that creates barriers and bondages instead of blessings and freedom in Christ.

In his book *"Kingdom, Grace, Judgement"* Robert Farrar Capon says, "The church is not in the religious business. It never has been and never will be. The church is in the Gospel-proclaiming business. It is not here to bring bad news but good news that while we were still sinners, Christ died for the ungodly. It is here for no religious purpose, only to announce the Gospel of free grace."

I was confused; although I was blessed and privileged to be in a great church where we saw results, I was still under pressure to perform. God is not impressed with our self-righteous works or any religious activity that is not Christ-centred. Christ's sacrificial death on the cross now supersedes Old Testament ceremonies and rigid religious rituals that were once sanctimonious but are now a load of legalistic baloney under the new covenant.

We read in Hebrews the blood of bulls and goats could not take away sin. "How much more shall the blood of Christ, who through the eternal Spirit offered Himself without spot to God, cleanse your conscience from dead works to serve the living God." Hebrews 9:14.

God has moved on from these ceremonial practices. As Christians, we now serve a living God. We are to be free from anything that looks like religion. We are to enjoy a loving relationship with Him because of His grace.

A love affair, not a religious one!

I thought our relationship with God should be more of a love affair, not a religious one.

Do we know God? Do we have a love relationship with Him, or are we like the Greeks in Athens, who were very religious?

Paul told them, "I have found an altar with this inscription: TO THE UNKNOWN GOD." Paul explained to them he knew who this unknown God was that they were honouring. He was the only true God, the creator of heaven and earth. Paul proclaimed the gospel and revealed that this God was Jesus Christ, who rose from the dead and would come again to judge the world.

Paul stated, *"He is not far from each one of us, for in Him we live and move and have our being."* Acts 17:22-28.

I knew who God was. I understood the gospel but needed to feel I was in Him, living and moving and having my being and identity in Him. I was not interested in developing a relationship with an unknown or indifferent God; I was looking for reality. Someone I could love, and they could love me back, a love affair, not a religious one. I longed to feel joined to Him, unlike a religious puppet on a string dancing to a performance tune.

Things were about to change!

Chapter 4

Waltzing to the tune of Grace

Yes, things were about to change.

I accepted an invitation to start a Bible College in Port Moresby, Papua New Guinea. I thought it would only be for one year, but we stayed for six years.

After feeling like a puppet on a string for some years in ministry in Melbourne, it was a life-changing experience.

The late John Pasterkamp was in charge of the work in Port Moresby. He was warm, friendly, open, and loving, as were the people.

For me, ministry in PNG was like a breath of fresh air. It was beautiful to experience such freedom in the Spirit. I felt like the puppet strings of the past were starting to be cut from my life as I began to understand God's grace. I was so free I felt like I was skipping in the Spirit.

It was like when I first met my wife, Caroline. We met at a Nurses' Ball in my hometown of Horsham. I was in my dinner suit, and she was in a lovely flowing red evening gown. She looked stunning. I asked her for a dance, and we waltzed and glided around the floor like we were floating on air. It felt so wonderful; love was in the air, and there was such freedom and joy as we waltzed the night away.

After that night, we kept dating, and after a whirlwind romance, we were married some six months later.

It was like I was waltzing to the tune of grace when I started to grow in the revelation of grace. I felt I was dancing in the Spirit. Anne Murray sings a lovely Country and Western love song, "Could I Have This Dance for the Rest of My Life." I wanted this grace experience for the rest of my life.

It was a love affair with God, not a religious one. It brought a new sense of freedom to my understanding of Christianity and a greater boldness to step out more in faith to serve the Lord in ministry. My relationship with God took on a whole new dimension.

When King David brought back the Ark of the Covenant, which represents the presence of the Lord, it says, ***"Then David danced before the Lord with all his might."*** 2 Samuel 6:14.

Joy flooded my heart; I no longer felt I had to perform or measure up to some religious standard set by the expectations of others. It was the grace of God in action. For me, it was true freedom in Christ.

Is God in love with you?

When I started dating my wife, Caroline, I was in love and longed to be with her constantly. Do you think God could be in love with you, wanting to spend time with you? I'm sure He does.

"I will not forget you. See, I have inscribed you on the palms of my hands." Isaiah 49:15:16.

I like to think of this as a wedding ring. He is always mindful of us because of His grace; He loves us and has inscribed us on the palms of His hands.

We are also the apple of His eye. We try to make all our children and grandchildren feel they are precious to us. They are all the apple of our eyes. We love them and want to watch over them.

"For he who touches you touches the apple of His eye." Zechariah 2:8. When we love someone, we want to defend and protect them.

God gets so joyful He sings over us.

"The Lord your God is in your midst, The Mighty One, will save; He will rejoice over you with gladness, He will quiet you with His love, He will rejoice over you with singing." Zephaniah 3:17.

These scriptures may refer to Christ, Israel, or the church. But because we are in Christ and joint heirs with Him. It also includes us as Christians.

No longer bullied

Because of His grace, I had a newfound freedom to be confident that I was led by the Holy Spirit and not bullied by the performance trap set by religious demands and expectations.

"For as many as are led by the Spirit of God, these are sons of God. For you did not receive the spirit of bondage again to fear, but you received the Spirit of adoption by whom we cry out "Abba Father" Romans 8:14-15.

Grace changed my thinking; I was confident that the Spirit was leading me. I became bolder and stepped out in faith to explore the dimensions and gifts of the Holy Spirit. Living in an atmosphere of love and grace helps us to learn how to walk in the Spirit. It also enables us to minister grace to others.

God's grace helped us survive in PNG and experience revival, where we saw many saved, healed, and delivered. They were exciting days with tremendous church growth and the gospel spreading throughout the nation.

It is the Spirit that gives life

Jesus said, *"It is the Spirit who gives life; the flesh profits nothing. The words that I speak to you are spirit, and they are life."* John 6:63.

It is the Spirit that gives life. As new covenant ministers, we depend upon the Holy Spirit's grace and power to impart life.

He has made us *"Sufficient as ministers of the new covenant not of the letter but of the Spirit; for the letter kills, but the Spirit gives life"* 2 Corinthians 3:6.

The Law, religion, legalism, and religious rituals could never make us sufficient as ministers. All they could do was keep us under bondage. For the letter kills, it does not produce life. So many Christians have this battle going on within them: bondage versus liberty. But it can only be by the Spirit that we are free from the bondage of legalism.

"Now the Lord is the Spirit; and where the Spirit of the Lord is, there is liberty." 2 Corinthians 3:17.

By the grace of God, only the Holy Spirit can liberate us from bondage and help us to minister freedom and grace to others. When we feel this kind of freedom, we seem to minister with a greater anointing and awareness of the presence and power of the Lord.

A remedy for the human race

Jesus performed many miracles during His ministry. He was compassionate, kind, loving, and gracious. But His ministry extended way past miracles. Jesus brought a remedy for the Human race to be cured of the most significant disease of all – sin. It was the greatest miracle of all.

So, He sacrificed His life by going to the cross to die for us and atone for our sins. He also rose again to secure eternal life and a place in heaven for us.

It is the unmerited favour of God which we have all received. It is called amazing grace. So Jesus did more than offer grace. He embodied grace.

I know when I have ministered on grace and people get a revelation of grace, it frees them from the feelings of not being worthy or any other form of condemnation the devil would try and dump on them. So they come in faith with an expectancy for healing and for God to meet their need.

Growing in Grace

I do not have all the answers to living in grace. I am still growing in grace and discovering more about grace. The bible indicates that this is a process.

"But grow in the grace and knowledge of our Lord Jesus Christ. To Him be glory both now and forever. Amen." 2 Peter 3:18.

So, in a way, as I write this book, I am still receiving revelation and understanding more about the grace of God. I suspect I will continue to do so for the rest of my life.

Chapter 5

The last remnants of religion

The last remnants of religion seem to lurk in dark corners, whereas authentic Christianity exposes the darkness by bringing things into the light.

While traveling in some parts of England and Ireland, we stopped to look at several old churches that were perfectly round without corners. It was so demons could not hide in dark corners. We may laugh at that, but it is not just demons that like darkness; it is also the evil deeds of men.

Jesus said, *"And this is the condemnation, that the light has come into the world, and men loved darkness rather than light because their deeds were evil."* John 3:19.

Before encountering Christ, we could apply this to the disciples, Pharisees, you, and me – who loved the darkness of our evil deeds, giving us a false sense of success. Our pride would rather not admit our failures, weaknesses, and need for grace. People are sometimes inclined to shun grace to hide their evil deeds.

In his book *"Kingdom, Grace, Judgment,"* Robert Farrar Capon makes an interesting observation -

"Grace doesn't sell; you can hardly give it away because it only works for losers, and nobody wants to stand in their line. The world of winners will buy caseloads of moral advice, grosses of guilt-edged prohibitions, skids of self-improvement techniques, and whole truckloads of transcendental hot air. But it will not buy free forgiveness because it threatens to let the riffraff into the Supper of the Lamb."

Yes, grace makes it possible for the so-called riffraff to enter. But we feel more comfortable being winners. People search for truth through self-improvement techniques and attractive religious activities because they promise success. But the question is, are they still covering their evil deeds?

If we want genuine success, we need to swallow our pride, humble ourselves, embrace the grace of God, and bring our weaknesses and failures to the light of the gospel for forgiveness and healing.

If we are prepared to do that, we are in a position to start exercising faith. By the grace of God, we can, by faith, accomplish great things.

Faith or failure?

We are inspired by the great exploits men and women accomplished *"by faith"* in Hebrews 11 until we come to verse

35, where we read of *"others"* who were not so fortunate.

"Others were tortured, not accepting deliverance, that they might obtain a better resurrection. Still, others had trials of mockings, scourgings, chains, and imprisonment. They were stoned, they were sawn in two, were tempted, were slain with the sword."….. "And all these, having obtained a good testimony through faith, did not receive the promise." Hebrews 11:35-39.

Although they may not have accomplished great things compared to others, they seemed to have failed. They still had a great testimony of faith. Despite what they faced and went through, they did not deny their faith in Christ and are more than worthy to be numbered among the great heroes of faith. They may have forfeited their lives but are guaranteed to be in the resurrection.

We now have a better deal

"… He is also mediator of a better covenant, which was established on better promises" Hebrews 8:6.

By the grace of God, it has made it so much easier for us because we have a much better deal.

Instead of grappling with remnants of the old covenant, we must embrace the Spirit of the new. What is the main difference between the old and new that affects our relationship with God today?

In Exodus 20, where God outlines the law, we continually

read, *"You shall,* or *"You shall not."* The emphasis is on *"You."* It is up to us to *"Do or not to Do."* It all depends on our ability to uphold the law. However, it is not that we negate all responsibility.

But when we come to the new covenant, the emphasis is on God taking the initiative. We continually read, *"I will."* What a difference! By the grace of God, we have all the help we need.

"For this is the covenant that 'I will' make with the house of Israel after those days, says the Lord: 'I will' put my laws in their mind and write them on their hearts, and 'I will' be their God, and they will be my people."…. "In that He says, a new covenant, He has made the first obsolete". Hebrews 8:10-13.

Because of Christ, God is now at work in our hearts and minds by the power of the Holy Spirit. The old religious ways of struggling to keep the law in our strength are over.

Our relationship with God relies on the grace of God and not on observing the law, which is now obsolete.

A deep hunger for God

Sometimes, it is hard to distinguish between a deep desire for more of God or a religious fervor. Although I was waltzing to the tune of grace on the mission field, a strange thing happened.

A few years before we left PNG, I felt led to fast and pray

out of a deep hunger for God and a need to seek direction for the future.

It was not my original intention, but I ended up fasting for forty days. To this day, I wonder if this was the last remnants of religion rising inside me to bite me or if it was my deep desire and hunger for more of God at the time. I want to think it was the latter.

I wrote a book using my journal as a platform during this experience as God poured out His Spirit. The book is titled *"Hungry for God,"* It consists of excerpts from a daily record of the insights and revelations I felt I had received, including many exciting adventures while on the mission field.

Fasting, to me, is one of many spiritual disciplines, like giving, bible study, prayer, worship, fellowship, and church attendance. These are all necessary for our spiritual development as we journey through life.

However, like most things, they can become unbalanced if taken to an extreme. If this fast were just a religious exercise, I would be in danger of becoming unstable mentally and physically. But by the grace of God, I survived and revived.

It was a monumental experience for me. I believe the Holy Spirit overruled the religious remnant that may have been raising its ugly head inside me and that everything was working together for good at the time as I sought the Lord.

What is your motivation?

The scriptures indicate that motivation is the key to any form of fasting. If you are fasting out of religious pride to exalt yourself, it is just spiritual pride and nothing more.

"Why have we fasted, they say, and you have not seen? Why have we afflicted our souls, and you take no notice." Isaiah 58:3.

It was because their heart was not in it. Their motive was not right, and God did not respond. However, in the same passage of scripture, God approves of the fast that He has ordained.

"Is not the fast that I have chosen: To loose the bonds of wickedness, to undo the heavy burdens, to let the oppressed go free, and that you break every yoke?" Verse 6.

If it is to feed the hungry, care for the poor, and cover the naked. The implication is if you fast with the right motive, God will hear you and respond to your prayers.

"Then you shall call, and the Lord will answer; You shall cry, and He will say, "Here I am." Verse 9.

Do you have to fast and pray long enough to hear from God? Is it essential? Is it a must?

The short answer is *"No,"* definitely not! Unless He is leading you to do so. Our relationship with God depends on grace and what Christ has done.

We do not have to do anything special to hear from God.

We cannot impress God by doing self-righteous religious works to get His attention.

Was the forty-day fast worth the experience? Yes, it gave me a great sense of achievement that once I put my mind to something, anything is possible.

It may sound like religious pride. But, by God's grace, I felt it helped me to fine-tune my relationship with the Holy Spirit and my sensitivity to the voice of the Lord.

Back to Australia

I accepted an invitation to return to Australia to become the senior pastor of a Church and Christian School in Lismore in the Northern Rivers of New South Wales. We loved Lismore and the church and stayed there for twenty-one years before semi-retiring to the Gold Coast.

However, I struggled with the message of grace. It was difficult initially because the church had been through a disappointing time, and many were hurting and resistant to change because the founding pastor had been stood down for impropriety.

I remember one of the first meetings in Lismore; as I got up to preach, the song leader whispered, "It's like mixing concrete up here." It is not what you want to hear when you are about to preach.

It was indicative of the condition of the church at the time. Despite having to work through several complex issues, it was not long before the atmosphere changed, and we enjoyed beautiful worship.

Ministering in Australia was far different from what I had experienced in PNG. I did not find the freedom and grace to minister as I wanted to; circumstances and the cynical Aussie culture seemed to hinder the freedom I was used to in PNG.

Love is the answer

When Jesus was asked, "Teacher, what is the great commandment in the law?" His answer summarised what the law was all about from a new covenant perspective.

"You shall love the Lord your God with all your heart, with all your soul, and with all your mind." "This is the first and great commandment." "And the second is like it: You shall love your neighbour as yourself." Matthew 22:36-39.

Interestingly, four of the Ten Commandments are about loving God. The last six Commandments deal with loving people (our neighbour). So Jesus sums up what fulfilling the law is all about – Love. We are to love God and our neighbour as ourselves. "Love" answers the question, "What is the great commandment in the law?" Love becomes the new commandment of the New Covenant. May the grace of God help us to love God and one another.

Jesus said, *"A new commandment I give to you, that you love one another; as I have loved you, that you also love one another. By this, all will know that you are My disciples if you have love for one another."* John 13:34-35.

Instead of religious politics and infighting, if only the world could see Christians and Churches loving God and one another, what an impact that would have on people.

You found your best friend

By the grace of God, you found your best friend, not a religion, when you came to faith in Christ.

In the context of Jesus giving His disciples the commandment to love one another, He makes an important statement.

"Greater love has no one than this, to lay down one's life for his friends. You are my friends if you do whatever I command you." John 15:13-14.

Yes, we are His friends if we are committed to following Him. He has already laid down His life for us, proving His friendship. I have many friends, and I am sure you do too, but I think of Him as my best friend.

Don Williams sings a Country and Western love song, but I like to think of it as a song unto the Lord as the words are appropriate. The chorus goes -

"You're my bread when I'm hungry

You're my shelter from troubled winds

You're my anchor in life's Ocean

But most of all, you're my best friend."

I love that, but most of all, you're my best friend. How wonderful to have God as your best friend.

How do I relate to God today?

You may be wondering how I relate to God today. Am I religious? Do I fast and pray a lot? I was conscious of hearing from God on the first day of my forty-day fast and probably could have stopped fasting after a few days.

I feel my relationship with God is far more relaxed today. I do little, if any, fasting. By the grace of God, I find He speaks to me as I pray and journal each morning or when I am shaving, in the shower, or driving the car. Maybe this is because I am relaxed and not busy doing other things. I have developed an expectation to hear from Him during these times.

So, these days, I am doing nothing remotely religious to hear from God. I am simply in tune with the Holy Spirit and listening for His voice, promptings, wisdom, and guidance.

I have been writing books since my retirement and have started on another one, *"The Ambiguous Kingdom."*

Chapter 6

Hallmarks of Grace in a Church

We all conjure up different images of what we think when we hear "Church." It is far more than a building with stained glass windows.

"How wonderful to know that Christianity is more than a padded pew or a dim cathedral, but that it is a real living daily experience which goes on from grace to grace." –Jim Elliot.

Yes, the church is more than a religious *"padded pew and a dim cathedral."* Unfortunately, when many think about church, that is all they have an image of rather than a church going on from grace to grace in the believer's life.

Someone asked me recently what I thought the church should look like if it displays hallmarks of grace. It is a good question, but everyone will have a slightly different opinion.

In other chapters, I have and will cover various aspects of what I think the church should look like. But, I would like to point out a few crucial qualities that should be hallmarks of grace.

- **Grace to handle opposition**

A church displaying grace will know how to survive and overcome opposition. By the grace of God, the church is here to stay.

Despite opposition from demonic forces and people, Jesus promised to build His church.

"I will build My church, and the gates of Hades will not prevail against it." Matthew 16:18.

There always seem to be issues within church life: the good, the bad, and the ugly. The church wrestles with spiritual forces who try to exploit this to create problems that cause division and disillusionment. As a result, there are a lot of hurt and wounded people who no longer attend church.

After fifty years, we recently participated in a Bible College reunion and were shocked as we talked to many ex-students who no longer attend church.

Some gave flimsy excuses, and some gave valid reasons, but as we listened, it became evident that there was a need for churches to show a lot more grace in trying to resolve issues. However, the church is here to stay, so we must soldier on.

- **Grace, not judgment**

We often judge others by their appearance and actions without knowing why they are the way they are.

I will share a story Charles Swindoll tells of how he spoke at a conference where he met a lovely couple.

The man was quiet; the wife was very exuberant. But he noticed that the man would immediately drop his head and sleep whenever he spoke during the conference.

Charles went into judgment mode, thinking they were unsuited and that she had married someone with no genuine interest in Christianity.

However, toward the end of the conference, the wife asked if she could speak with him privately.

He said, *"Of course,"* thinking she wanted to discuss a problem in their marriage. She said, *"I want to apologise for my husband." "He has terminal cancer, and the medication he takes makes him go to sleep."*

He was shocked that he had quickly judged this man without knowing his circumstances. He used this story to encourage believers not to judge others when they do not know the facts about them. If you have doubts about someone, make sure you investigate the circumstances.

- **Proclaiming a gospel of grace**

A church displaying grace will continually proclaim a gospel of grace. It is the essential message of the gospel. We are saved by grace and faith in Christ, not by being religious. It is the good news of the gospel. It is at the heart of the Christian message and offers eternal life and security for all who will respond.

Jesus said, *"The Spirit of the Lord is upon me because He has anointed me to preach the gospel to the poor. He sent me to heal the brokenhearted, to proclaim liberty to the captives, and recovery of sight to the blind, to set at liberty those who are oppressed, to proclaim the acceptable year of the Lord."* Luke 4:18.

Why did Jesus say God anointed Him? It was to preach the gospel. It is not just for us to have fuzzy church meetings as good as that may be. It is mainly for all those listed in the above scripture. It is a message that ministers grace to all who the enemy oppresses in some way.

- **Grace for the underdog**

A church displaying grace will love and embrace the underdog. By the grace of God, the church is to be like the Cave of Adullam. It was a place of safety for all those who were desperate.

To escape from Saul, David fled to the cave of Adullam. Many others joined him, making it a safe place for refugees and outcasts. David extended grace to everyone who came.

"So when his brothers and all his father's house heard it, they went down to him. And everyone who was in distress, everyone who was in debt, everyone

who was discontented gathered to him." 1 Samuel 22:1-2.

They were disconnected, desperate, distressed, and in debt, looking for contentment. I know some pastors who would rather see people like that join the church down the road. But they should be made welcome.

When the church extends grace, people discover a safe place to come and worship, where they feel loved and accepted and find contentment.

- **Grace for grasshoppers**

A church displaying grace will desire to overcome the grasshopper syndrome. Many Christians are intimidated by the fear of the world. Despite the size of your church, big or small, we should not fear reaching the world with the gospel, starting with our community.

The spies who went to spy out the promised land felt intimidated by the giants they saw and would eventually have to face.

"We saw the giants...and we were like grasshoppers in our own sight, and so we were in their sight." Numbers 13:33.

We may feel like grasshoppers sometimes because we are few compared to those who need to hear the gospel. We can be fearful of the giant task we face. By the grace of God, we are no longer grasshoppers in Christ; we are giant killers.

No matter what we face, we face it in Christ. We are overcomers despite the difficulties. We have everyday giants to overcome as we try to pay the rent or the mortgage, get food on the table, and stay fit and healthy. We should not fear but put our faith and trust in the Lord and His kingdom.

Jesus said, *"Do not fear, little flock, for it is your Father's good pleasure to give you the kingdom."* Luke 12:32.

The church must overcome the *"little flock"* image. We may feel outnumbered and insignificant compared to the overwhelming task of reaching the world with the gospel.

We serve an awesome God who has entrusted us with the greatest message the world can ever hope to hear. It is the only alternative to this world system. It is the kingdom of God.

It offers eternal security, something no other kingdom on earth can offer. We may feel intimidated, outnumbered, and overwhelmed by the great commission to go into all the world. But go, we must despite the odds.

- **Grace for your community**

    The church that displays grace will be a caring church, reaching out and helping its members and community somehow. By the grace of God, we need loving churches that are not just interested in how many people attend their church. We can easily focus on numbers, pour resources into doing that, and neglect people's needs.

Grace will produce a caring church. When Paul plans to send Timothy to the Philippians, he says, *"I have no one like-minded who will sincerely care for your state. All seek their own, not the things which are of Christ Jesus."* Philippians 2:20-21.

Paul was confident that Timothy would care for their state. It means he would do more than preach; he would also care for their needs. This caring attitude needs to extend into the community.

Many churches that show grace run op-shops, soup kitchens, or programs to feed the poor. Some provide Christian education through schools. Others are involved with community organisations that help in different ways during natural disasters.

A caring church that displays grace will be a loving church that wants to reach out to all.

BUT FOR THE GRACE OF GOD GO I

Chapter 7

Grace to forgive

Grace has enabled us to put our faith in Christ, who shed His blood on the cross for our forgiveness.

"In Him, we have redemption through His blood, the forgiveness of sins, according to the riches of His grace." Ephesians 1: 7.

We must be mindful of this when forgiving others who have mistreated us. God extended grace, love, and mercy to us. Can we do the same, especially to those who have hurt or abused us?

A lack of forgiveness comes in different ways: a breakup in a relationship, a betrayal, family disputes, or some hurt that has sown a seed of bitterness and resentment.

At some point, we must let go of the past hurts and begin to heal, but the decision to forgive is often the starting point and will eventually lead to a happier, more fulfilled, and more fruitful life.

A seedbed for bitterness

If we hold onto unforgiveness, it can be a seedbed for bitterness and hinder our ability to love.

"We must develop and maintain the capacity to forgive. He who is devoid of the power to forgive is devoid of the power to love." -Martin Luther King Jr.

Sometimes, people say, *"I will never forgive them for what they have done to me."* Others state, *"I can forgive, but I will never forget."* If we have this attitude, we can harbour bitterness and not be accessible to love until we forgive.

I was counseling a lady with an arthritic condition in her shoulder who could hardly lift it. I asked her how long she had been like this. She said ever since my husband cheated on me and we separated.

I asked, *"Have you forgiven him?"* She said, *"Yes, but I will never forget what he has done to me."* As I dug deeper, it became evident that there was a root of bitterness toward him. I led her in prayer for forgiveness and inner healing. When she stood up to leave, she lifted her arm from the shoulder and found freedom of movement.

A few weeks later, she was claiming that God had healed her. Somehow, there seemed to be a connection between forgiveness, inner healing, and physical healing. True forgiveness is about showing grace to forgive everyone, including those who have wounded us.

Grace to keep on forgiving

The law required sacrifices for forgiveness. There is no direct scripture that I am aware of to indicate how many times you were to forgive, but by inference, there seems to be a limit to forgiveness under the old covenant. The implication is that you were to forgive someone three times and, if you were generous, a fourth time. (Job 33:29, Amos 2:6).

So when Peter asks Jesus how many times you should forgive someone, Peter answers the question before Jesus can answer. Peter says, *"Up to seven times,"* thinking he was highly generous according to the old covenant.

"Then Peter came to Him and said, "Lord, how often shall my brother sin against me, and I forgive him?" "Up to seven times." Jesus said to him, "I do not say to you up to seven times, but up to seventy times seven." Matthew 18:21-22.

By saying up to seventy times seven, Jesus implies that Peter is not even close. It is a symbolic number that means there is no end to forgiving someone. It is like grace extended over and over again. It is unlike the law that indicates enough is enough. Grace encourages us to keep on forgiving those who have offended us.

So, if we still resent them, we must forgive them repeatedly until it is no longer an issue for us.

A parable about forgiveness

Immediately after Jesus answers Peter with "Up to seventy times seven," he tells the parable of the unforgiving servant. The servant was in debt to his master and could not repay him. He asked the master to be lenient with him.

"The master of the servant was moved with compassion, released him, and forgave him the debt." Matthew 18:27.

But then the servant went and found those who owed him a debt and demanded that they pay him. When they could not pay him, he had them thrown into prison. He did not forgive them of their debt.

When the servant's master found out, he said, *"You wicked servant! I forgave you all that debt because you begged me. Should you not also have had compassion on your fellow servant, just as I had pity on you?"* And his master was angry and delivered him to the torturers until he should pay all that was due to him. *"So my heavenly Father also will do to you if each of you, from his heart, does not forgive his brother his trespasses."* Matthew 18:32-35.

So, we can see how important it is to forgive because God has been gracious to us by having compassion on us and forgiving us. We must, therefore, forgive and keep on forgiving others.

The closer we are to someone, especially another Christian friend or church leader, who has hurt or betrayed us somehow, the harder it is to forgive them.

David said, *"For it is not an enemy who reproaches me; Then I could bear it. Nor is it one who hates me who has exalted himself against me; then I could hide from him. But it was you, a man my equal, my companion and my acquaintance, we took sweet counsel together and walked to the house of God in the throng."* Psalm 55:12-14.

Some Commentaries say David referred to Ahithophel, a close associate and friend at some stage. For me, forgiving another leader or close friend who offended me is tough. But by the grace of God, forgive them, I must.

Revenge is not an option

We may become angry with those who have offended or abused us. The natural human response when we have been hurt, used, or taken advantage of is to seek revenge.

Again, according to the law, it was an eye for an eye and a tooth for a tooth. You were entitled to retaliate with an equal response if someone were to rough you up or mistreat you. But according to Jesus, this is not an option. We are to forgive not only our brethren but also our enemies.

Jesus said, *"Whoever slaps you on the right cheek, turn the other to him also."…. "You have heard it said, You shall love your neighbour and hate your enemy. "But I say to you, love your enemies, bless those who curse you, do good to those who hate you, and pray for those who spitefully use you and persecute you."* Matthew 5:38-44.

You might be thinking, "Well, that is not fair." They should not be able to get away with it. Why do we have to be so gracious and loving toward them? It is not up to us to seek revenge; just let go and let God deal with them.

"Vengeance is Mine, I will repay," says the Lord. Therefore, *"If your enemy is hungry, feed him; if he is thirsty, give him a drink; for in so doing you will heap coals of fire upon his head."* Romans 12:19-20.

Avoid Spiritual abuse

Is it possible to forgive those who have abused us spiritually or physically in some way? Can we extend grace to them? We know abuse can cover many aspects of life, including spiritual, emotional, sexual, physical, verbal, and financial.

Usually, *'spiritual'* abuse is more subtle and can come through extreme misguided enthusiasm.

As a result of different forms of spiritual abuse, people can become disillusioned, suspicious, hurt, and even stop attending church.

It is hard to forgive and extend grace to those who have abused us. We may have to work on it, but it is better to avoid spiritual abuse in the first place.

In medical terms, we often say prevention is better than

the cure. What can we do to prevent spiritual abuse?

A good thing to do is ask yourself, what would Jesus do? Would He behave this way? Does this align with the character teaching of Jesus?

We need to become fruit inspectors.

Jesus said, *"Beware of false prophets, who come to you in sheep's clothing, but inwardly they are ravenous wolves. You will know them by their fruits. Do men gather grapes from thornbushes or figs from thistles? Even so, every good tree bears good fruit, but a bad tree bears bad fruit. A good tree cannot bear bad fruit, and a bad tree can not bear good fruit."* Matthew 7:17-18.

We also have a list of what the fruit of the Spirit should look like. *"But the fruit of the Spirit is love, joy, peace, longsuffering, kindness, goodness, faithfulness, gentleness, self-control. Against such, there is now law."* Galatians 5:22-23.

We have all been guilty of putting Charisma before Character. Let us be wise enough to examine the fruit of other Christians, particularly those in ministry.

BUT FOR THE GRACE OF GOD GO I

Chapter 8

Parables of Grace and Truth

Jesus spoke in parables. A parable is a short and simple story that teaches us a lesson. Jesus was a great storyteller who used parables to convey grace and truth. People find it easy to remember stories.

The first time an experienced minister heard me preach, he took me aside and said, *"Your word was great from a scriptural perspective. But you need to tell some stories or give illustrations people can relate to, for they are like windows that let in the light to clarify your message."* That was a great word of advice, which I have tried to put into practice. Everyone loves a good story; I know I do, and I suspect you do.

When Jesus spoke in parables, He told stories that gave understanding and revelation concerning the things of God.

"All these things Jesus spoke to the multitude in parables; and without a parable He did not speak to them, that it might be fulfilled which was spoken by the

prophet, saying; "I will open My mouth in parables; I will utter things kept secret from the foundation of the world." Matthew 13:34-35.

Although parables were simple stories, sometimes people struggled to understand the meaning. But Jesus would explain them to His disciples privately.

"But without a parable, He did not speak to them. And when they were alone, He explained all things to His disciples." Mark 4:34.

The Parables highlight Grace

Although the parables give us a balance of grace and truth, they seem to lean towards grace.

Maybe this was because Jesus dealt so much with the Pharisees and Scribes, who were intent on upholding the law. They appear to have no compassion or understanding of the grace of God. So Jesus seems to emphasise God's grace in many of the parables.

For example, three parables in Luke 15 portray the grace of God. So, to make it easy to follow, we will examine each one consecutively and expound on them, highlighting the grace of God, even though the word 'grace' is not mentioned.

The lost sheep -

Jesus told this parable after the judgemental Pharisees and scribes criticised Him for receiving tax collectors and sinners and eating with them. So Jesus spoke this parable to them.

"What man of you, having a hundred sheep, if he loses one of them, does he not leave the ninety-nine in the wilderness, and go after the one that is lost until he finds it. And when he finds it he lays it over his shoulder, rejoicing. And when he comes home he calls his friends and neighbours saying to them. Rejoice with me, for I have found my sheep, which was lost! I say to you that likewise there will be more joy in heaven over one sinner who repents than over ninety-nine just persons who need no repentance." Luke 15:3-7.

The religious leaders were more concerned about their success, superiority, self-righteous works, and upholding the law than they were for the salvation of lost sinners.

We see the heart of Jesus, that He came to save the lost. He is more concerned about extending grace to the lost. A good shepherd will not only want to feed and tend the flock but also go after the one who has gone astray and become lost.

We could spend much time expounding 'lostness' concerning these parables. However, we would be missing a significant point that Jesus is making. That is one of joy. The parable says, **"Rejoice with me, for I have found my lost sheep."** After Jesus describes joy here on earth, He pushes the parable to heaven, saying, **"There is great joy not only on earth but also in heaven."** Jesus concludes by highlighting joy.

The parable also portrays the lack of joy, love, and grace shown by the Pharisees and Scribes toward the lost and reveals how God extends grace to them and is overjoyed when they respond. However, the truth of the parable is that the sinner still needs to repent of their sin and turn to Christ. It is prevenient grace that enables them to do this.

The lost coin –

Jesus follows on with another parable in the same vane as the lost sheep dealing with that which is lost.

Jesus said, *"Or what woman, having ten silver coins, if she loses one coin, does not light a lamp sweet the house, and search carefully until she finds it? And when she has found it. She calls her fiends and neighbours together, saying rejoice with me, for I have found the piece which was lost! Likewise, I say to you, there is joy in the presence of the angels of God over one sinner who repents."* Luke 15:8-10.

Once again, we see the urgency to drop everything and search for that which is lost. That which was lost becomes the priority.

When the woman finds the coin, she calls her friends and neighbours and invites them to rejoice, for she has found the lost coin. Once again, we see an emphasis on rejoicing.

Again, Jesus takes it into heaven and concludes, *"Thus I say to you there is joy before the angels of God over one sinner who repents."*

Angels are probably involved in bringing people to Christ without us realising it. But the responsibility here lies with the woman to search until she finds that which is lost.

It is a lesson for all churches and Christians that our priority is to reach the lost with the gospel. Nothing brings greater joy than to see the lost turn to Christ.

The lost son –

Jesus follows on with another parable about a lost son. Interestingly, the parable mentions two sons, with the main story directed at the lost son.

"A certain man had two sons. And the younger of them said to his father, give me the portion of goods that falls to me. So, he divided to them his livelihood. And not many days after, the younger son gathered all together, journeyed to a far country, and there wasted his possessions on prodigal living." Luke 15:11-13.

The prodigal son not only went astray, but he made a complete mess of his life. He squandered his inheritance, lost everything, and ended up eating food fed to the pigs to survive.

He eventually came to his senses and said, *"I will arise and go to my father and will say to him, Father, I have sinned against heaven and before you."* Verse 18.

When he returned home, he found his father was waiting for him, took him in as his son, and put on a party to welcome him home. It was to be a grand celebration of joy.

The elder brother came home, but instead of joining the party, he became angry and acted self-righteously, explaining to the father that he had been faithful all this time and that if anyone deserved a party, it was him. His attitude was indicative of the self-righteous Pharisees and Scribes.

The Father typifies our Heavenly Father, who has a passion for the lost and extends grace to those who go astray and make a mess of their lives.

These parables of *'lostness'* are about God's grace and the fruit of grace when sinners turn to Christ, which is joy. The parables are not about improving ourselves by becoming religious and self-righteous through our good works to find salvation.

These parables are about the grace of God and grace alone that enables us to come boldly back to a loving God. We were lost, but once we come to our senses and repent, we can return to a loving Father waiting for us. We should not be afraid of God and hide like Adam and Eve did when they knew they had sinned. It is better to rely on the grace of God that leads us to a loving Father.

Workers in the vineyard -

Another parable of grace paints a similar picture, only more aligned with the elder brother's attitude in the lost son story. It is that of the workers in the vineyard. The landowner went out early in the morning to hire workers for the vineyard.

"He had agreed with the labourers for a denarius a day and sent them into his vineyard." Matthew 20:2.

But as the day went by, he needed more labourers and hired some at the third, sixth, ninth, and eleventh hour.

When they came to get paid, the ones hired at the eleventh hour also received a Danarius, the same as those hired at the first hour of the day. So what did they do? It's the same as what you and I would have done. They complained that it was unfair because they had worked a full day while the others only worked one hour.

He answered, *"Friend, I am doing you no wrong. Did you not agree with me for a denarius? ...Is it not lawful for me to do what I wish."* Verse 13-15.

We can interpret this in different ways, but for me, it speaks of those who labour long for the Lord and may take a pharisaical attitude that they are more worthy and deserve more than the sinner who is saved by grace at the last minute, like the dying thief on the cross. Yes, we will eventually all receive a reward for serving the Lord. But when it comes to salvation, we can do nothing to earn salvation because we are all saved by grace and grace alone.

The absence of joy

It is noticeable that there is a significant lack of joy where religion without grace is dominant.

I had an old auntie who was a spinster. She was a strict Catholic and would religiously walk a mile to church, rain, hail, or shine almost daily for mass. She was committed to her church. But she was also very religious and self-righteous but

But for the GRACE of God go I

seemed to have no joy whatsoever. She could be pretty mean. No matter what opinion you had, she was always right.

When I was in my early teens, before becoming a Christian, she almost put me off Christianity. She was more of an advertisement for religion than she was for Christianity.

I do not want to be too hard on her; maybe her prayers helped lead to my salvation. But the point is religion kills love and joy. Grace can be the seedbed for love and joy and the blessing of the Lord.

Chapter 9

His Grace is sufficient

We have a potential problem!

If God loves us so much and has extended His grace to us, why are we sometimes left hanging without a solution or an answer when we face unresolved difficulties?

What if your prayers seem to be delayed or denied? Or if God even says *"No,"* How will you respond? I know I get frustrated.

What did the apostle Paul do? There was a time when Paul had a "thorn in the flesh," but we do not know what it was. There was some ailment he was battling in his body. It was a messenger from Satan to buffet him. Paul thought it was to keep him humble because of the revelations he had received. He wanted to get rid of it. So he prayed God would take it away. Not once, but three times.

"Concerning this thing, I pleaded with the Lord three

times that it might depart from me." 1 Corinthians 12:8.

The only answer he got was probably one he did not expect, and I suspect that we also get the same response when we are suffering in some way and our prayers are unanswered. God gave Paul this revelation –

"My grace is sufficient for you, for My strength is made perfect in weakness." 1 Corinthians 12:9.

What is your thorn in the flesh?

Do you feel you have a thorn in the flesh? Is it some buffeting from Satan? Is it something that ails you, a sickness, an infirmity? Have you been hurt or abused by a person? A broken relationship? The loss of a loved one? Is there something that has hindered you and caused you even to question your faith in God?

You may be limping through life because of some thorn in the flesh. It is like a stabbing pain, something you are desperate to get rid of. You seek counsel and comfort from friends. You seek medical advice. There seems to be no answer. Whatever it is, you have prayed about it, but it lingers.

The only answer you seem to get is, "His grace is sufficient for you." Which is like God reassuring you that you can get through this.

A humbling experience

I will never forget my first trip to India. I have probably told this story before, but it is worth repeating. I went to minister in a Bible School in Hyderabad.

It was a humiliating experience. A few days before leaving Australia, I tore my left calf muscle playing tennis, and as a precaution against disease, received injections in the left arm and left buttock. I was sore and walked with a lop-sided limp as I boarded the plane.

When I finally arrived at the Bible School, it was evening, and I went straight to bed. The following day, when I woke up and looked in the mirror, I had a swollen left eye. I could not believe what was looking back at me. Something bit me during the night. The students expected to be taught by this experienced missionary and man of faith. As I limped into the classroom, I was not surprised by their stunned look of disbelief.

But to make things worse, the following day, I woke up and had to rush to the toilet with what they call "Deli Belly" in India. Several times, I had to excuse myself from lectures and hurry to the bathroom.

I felt the devil was buffeting me. I started rebuking the enemy and cried out to the Lord for healing. All I got was, *"My grace is sufficient for you."* In retrospect, I think I went to India with a lot of pride, thinking I had all the answers. Maybe the Lord was keeping me humble.

The students and staff were very gracious and concerned for my welfare. The principal of the Bible School came and said to me, "We will get the village doctor to come and look at you." I thought to myself, the village doctor, is that a good idea? Anyway, the village doctor came and gave me a massive injection. To my surprise, it worked. I was better within hours, except for the limp. I continued for another week of lectures and ministry and ended up having a very profitable time.

His enabling power

Paul expounds grace as the enabling power of God that will carry him through difficult times.

Grace is a bit like an extra shot in the arm or a booster that gives you a dose of patience and endurance, which we need for a breakthrough. "And so, after he had patiently endured, he obtained the promise." Hebrews 6:15.

It is not over when we face hard times; you are never defeated; it is a test of faith. We must patiently endure, and then God gives us the grace, His "enabling power," to hang in there and win through to eventual victory.

I was distraught when I was diagnosed with prostate cancer and faced six weeks of radiation treatment and hormone therapy. I did not want to proceed with the treatment because of the potential side effects. I felt the Lord say that His grace was sufficient for me and that I would get through it because He was with me. So, I went ahead with it, although I did not enjoy the treatment.

Thankfully, the side effects were minor. I endured, and His grace was sufficient for me. The result is that there is now no sign of cancer. Praise God!

A touch of humility helps

Paul interprets this "thorn in the flesh" in the light of all the revelations he has received. He feels it is to keep him humble, and if he needs this weakness to make him strong in the Spirit, then his attitude is to bring it on. Grace will enable him to handle it.

We read in the book of James –

"God resists the proud but gives grace to the humble." James 4:6.

Humility attracts the grace of God like a magnet. However, pride has the opposite effect; it repels the grace of God and makes us vulnerable to deception, temptation, and rebellion. It is why Paul embraces that His grace is sufficient for him.

Jesus gives us a picture of the difference between pride and humility when he tells of the parable of the Pharisee and the tax collector. They both went up to the temple to pray.

"The Pharisee stood and prayed thus with himself, God, I thank you, I am not like other men – extortioners, unjust, adulterers, or even as this tax collector. I fast twice a week; I give tithes of all that I possess. And the tax collector standing afar off would not so much as raise his eyes to heaven but beat his breast, saying, "Be merciful to me, a sinner." Luke 18:11-13.

The Pharisee displayed such religious pride, big-noting himself for his religious works and exalting himself as superior to the tax collector. The tax collector showed humility and asked for forgiveness for his sins.

Jesus was more impressed with the tax collector's humility than the Pharisee and his religious pride.

"I tell you this man went down to his house justified rather than the other, for everyone who exalts himself will be humbled, and he who humbles himself will be exalted." Verse 14.

It is like God is sometimes saying, *"Back off, it is okay, I am in control, My grace is enough, it is all you need, it is sufficient to get you through this."*

Learn to be content

Grace will help us to learn to be content. We may not get the miracle we expect or what we pray for, but we need to learn to be content no matter what we may be going through.

The Apostle Paul puts it this way, *"I have LEARNED in whatever state I am in to be content. I have LEARNED both to be full and to be hungry, both to abound and to suffer need. I can do ALL things through Christ who strengthens me."* Philippianes 4:11-13.

It is not natural for us to be content all the time. It is something we have to work on by the grace of God. Paul had to learn to be content in whatever state he was in. He can do it because Christ gives him the strength to handle every situation.

I recently listened to John Denver sing an old country and western song. A part of the chorus goes - *"Some days are diamonds; some days are stones."*

We all have days like that; some are great days, like diamonds, and others are not so good, like stones, but no matter what kind of day you are experiencing, His grace is sufficient for you.

BUT FOR THE GRACE OF GOD GO I

Chapter 10

The manifold Grace Gifts of God

What is meant by manifold grace? It simply refers to the many reflective and fascinating facets of the grace of God.

It is like holding a beautiful diamond to the light and turning it around to see it sparkle. Some time ago, we visited the Argyle diamond mine in a remote part of Western Australia. The beauty of these diamonds blew us away. So did the price; there was no way we could afford them.

Australia is also famous for multi-coloured opals, which are stunning. When held to the light, they reflect many brilliant colours.

We visited the renowned opal fields at Lightning Ridge in outback New South Wales. We had to admire the exquisite beauty of these opals but not their price, as they were also so expensive. Some miners spend their whole lives chasing these glorious stones.

Grace is not something you must dig for or spend your life chasing; it is a beautiful gift worth more than opals and diamonds. It is freely given to us by God and not something we must pay for or earn.

Manifold grace gifts

To lay a foundation, we must examine what the apostle Peter mentions in the following scripture.

"As each one has received a gift, minister it to one another, as good stewards of the manifold grace of God." 1 Peter 4:10.

Peter is saying all this in the context of urgency, that time is running out, and there is a great need to stop grumbling and start loving one another because love covers a multitude of sins. So start ministering to one another in love.

The most effective way for them to do this (and for us) is by exercising the spiritual gifts that God has given to each person.

As 'each one' has received a gift. It would indicate that all believers have a gift given by the grace of God. We acquired this by grace, and it is by grace that we use it. We have not earned this gift or the right to use it, for it is given and operated through us entirely by grace through the power of the Holy Spirit.

In discussions with some key leaders in PNG, they said, "If you ever write another book, please include a section on all the Spiritual Gifts." Well, here it is!

I would suggest there are three significant areas concerning gifts that we should examine. They are all a result of the grace of God –

1. Fivefold ministry gifts

The fivefold ministry gifts are not earned but given by Christ. They are ministry gifts capable of ministering to the whole Body of Christ to build up believers and bring them to a place of maturity in Christ.

"But to each one of us grace was given according to the measure of Christ's gift."…. "And He Himself gave some to be apostles, some prophets, some evangelists, and some pastors and teachers, for the equipping of the saints for the work of ministry, for the edifying of the body of Christ." Ephesians 4:7,11-12.

The five listed above are –

1. **Apostles** – Are sent out by God to proclaim the gospel. They are often pioneers or visionaries who plant churches. They can also help establish existing churches. They have an authority that others recognise.

2. **Prophets** – They can prophesy and bring a timely word of truth to help steer the believers to follow the Lord. They are to do this in a way that encourages the whole church.

3. **Evangelists** – Are those who can gather a crowd and

present the gospel to those who have not heard it. They are often exceptional speakers who compel people to turn to Christ.

4. **Pastors** – They feed and shepherd the flock in the local church. They care for the people and tend to their needs. They are wise and preach and teach the word of God. They guard or watch over the flock to protect and guide the church.

5. **Teachers** – Are sometimes theologians. They can expound and explain the truth revealed in the word. They often have a heart for equipping people and feel at home in a Bible School. They love teaching students or believers in the local church.

All these ministry gifts are by the grace of God to people whom God selects to bring His church to maturity. Christ chooses the person, and the Holy Spirit does the enabling. We recognise them by their fruit.

2. Motivational gifts

To avoid confusion, I will call them motivational gifts given to us by the grace of God. They match our personality, spiritual gifting, and calling in life.

These gifts are not to be confused with the fivefold ministry gifts or spiritual gifts, although there will be some overlapping with these gifts.

"Having then gifts differing according to the grace

given to us, let us use them: if prophecy let us prophesy in proportion to our faith, or in ministry, let us use it in ministering; he who teaches, in teaching; he who exhorts, in exhortation; he who gives, with liberality; he who leads, with diligence; he who shows mercy, with cheerfulness." Romans 12:6-8.

I will list the seven gifts mentioned, and to help you identify your gift, I will put in brackets how you may react if you imagine sitting at a table with a group of people and someone spilled their food on the floor. Your reaction may help you identify your gift.

1. **Prophecy** – The ability to speak prophetically (you would have much to say and question how this happened and who was responsible).

2. **Ministry** – The ability to serve others (you would grab a mop and start cleaning up the mess).

3. **Teaching** – The ability to explain truth (you would try to figure out how it happened and then give a detailed account to everyone).

4. **Exhorting** – The ability to encourage others (you would probably say there is plenty more and laugh it off with a joke).

5. **Giving** – This speaks of generosity by giving (you would probably offer them your food).

6. **Leadership** – The ability to lead others (you would

start organising others to clean up the mess).

7. **Mercy** – To show mercy to those in need (you would put your arm around them, comfort them, and tell them not to worry).

The above examples in brackets are only a guide as to how you may react if someone spills their food at the table. It may not be the best way to identify your gifting, but it should help.

These are essential gifts given to us by the grace of God. Life will be much less stressful when we operate in the gift that fits us. We all have one that seems more prominent. However, they may overlap at times.

If you can identify your gift and that of others, it will help you to understand yourself and others as to how you and others think and do what you do the way you do it.

3. Spiritual gifts

Spiritual gifts are given to us by the grace of God. The word gift in Greek is 'charisma,' a gift given gratuitously or by grace, as the Spirit distributes to everyone as He wills.

"The manifestation of the Spirit is given to each one for the profit of all: for to one is given a word of wisdom through the Spirit, to another the word of knowledge through the same Spirit, to another faith by the same Spirit, to another gifts of healings by the same Spirit, to another the working of miracles, to another prophecy, to another discerning of spirits, to another

different kinds of tongues, to another the interpretation of tongues." 1 Corinthians 12:7-10.

There are nine supernatural gifts of the Holy Spirit; they are not natural abilities. They are as follows –

1. **A word of wisdom** – A wise and timely word that usually helps us to make a decision and act upon it.

2. **A word of knowledge** – It reveals concealed Knowledge that outlines the facts of a given situation.

3. **Faith** – Imparted for a given need at a particular time.

4. **Gifts of Healing** – Gifts plural - for various healings (e.g., Deaf ears to be opened, etc.)

5. **Working of miracles** – For demonstrating the miracle-working power of God.

6. **Prophecy** – Speaking and prophecying for the edification of believers.

7. **Discerning of spirits** – The ability to identify and distinguish various kinds of spirits.

8. **Different kinds of tongues** – Speaking mysteries in the Spirit to God and for self-edification.

9. **Interpretation of tongues** – interpreting mysteries in the Spirit for all believers to understand and be edified.

These are gifts given by the grace of God to different individuals but by the same Spirit. It is the Holy Spirit working for the benefit of believers and the church.

For example, during my time in ministry, I found that by the grace of God, I would function more in the gift of a word of wisdom or knowledge and occasionally a prophetic word. It was evident when I ministered with such freedom in PNG. I have told this story before, but it is worth repeating as it is one I will never forget.

I was speaking at a series of meetings in Lae. It was Saturday night, and when I gave an altar call, I had a 'Word of Knowledge' I said, "There is a young man in the foyer. God has His hand on your life, and you need to come forward and receive Christ as your Saviour." This young man went away, but he kept thinking about it. He came back the next night, and again, when it came to the altar call, I said, "The same young man I mentioned last night is back in the foyer, standing in the same spot; God is giving you another chance to come forward and receive Christ." This time, he came forward and committed his life to Christ.

Many years later, I met this young man at a conference. He had become the overseer of several churches in his province.

The gifts of the Holy Spirit differ from the fruit of the Spirit. The fruit of the Spirit has more to do with our character development and maturity, a process that becomes evident as we learn to walk in the Spirit. (Galatians 5: 22-25).

All gifts are an expression of the manifold grace of God. We can not earn them, and we do not deserve them. They are given unconditionally, freely, and instantly as the need arises.

Chapter 11

Who has bewitched you?

Paul is disappointed and upset when he writes to the Galatians to rebuke them for being so easily deceived and led astray.

"O foolish Galatians! Who has bewitched you that you should not obey the truth, before whose eyes Jesus Christ was clearly portrayed among you as crucified?" Galatians 3: 1.

We see how bold and fearless Paul was in confronting them. Calling people *'foolish'* and *'bewitched'* is not how to make friends and develop good relationships. If Paul were alive today, I don't think he would want to read Dale Carnegie's book, *"How to Win Friends and Influence People."*

But Paul had reason to rebuke them for so quickly wandering away from the truth that he had already imparted to the believers when he planted the church in Galatia. Paul is saying this in the context of them being under a spell of deception and led astray from the gospel of grace he had initially given them.

"I marvel at you turning away so soon from Him who called you in the grace of Christ to a different gospel. ... There are some who trouble you and want to pervert the gospel of Christ." Galatians 1:6-7.

Confusion in Galatia

Paul said, *"There are some who trouble you."* Who were they? Judaisers who added Jewish customs and laws to the gospel Paul had taught. They were telling the Christians they still needed to become like Jews. For example, men need to get circumcised. It was causing confusion among Christians in Galatia.

There seems to be an identity crisis. Who were Christians? Did they need to become like Jews and adhere to circumcision? No, they were a new creation in Christ, a completely new identity.

"For in Christ Jesus, neither circumcision nor uncircumcision avails anything but a new creation." Galatians 6:15.

All that matters is that we are a new creation.

Despite having begun their Christian journey on the proper foundation of grace and faith in Christ for salvation, Judaisers encouraged them to revert to areas of the law to become acceptable Christians.

We read in chapter two that James, Peter, and, to some

extent, Barnabas were supportive of some of the Jews who were demanding that the Gentiles submit to parts of the law of Moses. Paul is not impressed and publicly confronts Peter, saying that this is not right and that the only way to be justified is by faith in Christ, not the works of the law.

As a result, they had drifted away from the truth. They thought God's grace was insufficient, and they had to add parts of the law to the simplicity of the gospel. Paul implies they were under a spell of deception. That is why he asks, *"O foolish Galatians! Who has bewitched you?"*

Witchcraft and sorcery

When we were on the mission field in PNG, witchcraft and sorcery were still practiced in some areas, and we would pray and bind the influence of these spiritual forces before entering a village with the gospel.

One missionary in a remote place told me how he woke up in the middle of the night, and a demon in the form of an old man with dreadlocks was standing at the end of his bed, who said to him, *"You must leave this area because these people have been under my spell for centuries."* The missionary rebuked the demon and declared, *"No, they do not belong to you; the blood of Christ has redeemed them."* He commanded the demon in the name of Jesus to leave the area, and for months following, revival broke out.

Those who practiced witchcraft and sorcery in these areas were overbearing and liked to control and manipulate people.

Paul implies this when he says, *"Who has bewitched*

you?" Who is trying to control and manipulate you to deceive you?

A revelation that changed history

Martin Luther had submitted to the religious rituals of Catholicism and spent a lot of time doing penance until he read the book of Galatians.

He received a revelation that changed the course of history. Christians were "justified by faith" in Christ through the finished work of the cross. They did not have to try to keep specific laws or do penance and punish themselves because they failed to comply with all the rules.

Martin Luther's teachings on the Reformation can be found in three *"Solas," Sola Gratia, Sola Fide, and Sola Scriptura* – by grace alone, faith alone, and scripture alone.

However, the Galatians did not fully embrace the revelation that the *"just shall live by faith."* They were confused by the Judaisers who infiltrated their ranks and reverted to some Jewish laws instead of continuing to lay hold of the gospel of grace given to them by Paul.

A great foundation

Paul laid an excellent foundation for the Galatians by expounding the gospel of grace that a person was justified through their faith in Christ and not through the law.

Some of the things Paul had explained to them–

1. The gospel of grace was a revelation.
2. Christians are under a covenant of grace
3. They are no longer under the law
4. Their faith in Christ justifies them.
5. It is the work of the Spirit, not the flesh.

In laying this foundation, Paul had taught on the finished work of the cross.

"...Before whose eyes Jesus Christ was clearly portrayed among you as crucified." Galatians 3: 1.

The cross had become the focal point for the early Christians. Through the shed blood of Jesus, a person could find forgiveness of sin by putting their faith in Christ, who had now finished the work of atonement for sins.

No longer were they required to uphold the law for their salvation.

It was the grace of God; Salvation had become a gift, not something you had to earn by your self-righteous, religious good works.

Paul asks questions

Paul asks the church in Galatia several questions –

"Did you receive the Spirit by the works of the law or by the hearing of faith?" Verse 2.

Again, in verse 3, *"Are you so foolish? Having begun in the Spirit, are you now being made perfect by the flesh?"*

Again, in verse 5, *"Therefore He who supplies the Spirit to you and works miracles among you does He do it by the works of the law or by the hearing of faith?"* The answers are obvious: it was by faith, not the works of the law, but the work of the Spirit.

Paul eventually summarises these questions by pointing the Judaisers to the father of their faith, Abraham.

"Therefore, know only those who are of faith are sons of Abraham. The scripture, foreseeing that God would justify the Gentiles by faith, preached the gospel to Abraham." Galatians 3:7-8.

Paul explains, *"To Abraham and his Seed were the promises made."* He does not say, *"And to seeds"* as of many, but as of one, *"And to your Seed,"* who is Christ. Verse 16. And again in verse 29, *"And if you are Christ's, then you are Abraham's seed, and heirs according to the promise."*

Opposition to the gospel of grace

Jesus faced opposition to the gospel of grace similar to that of the Galatians. Judaisers confronted him, and the battle between law and grace, bondage and freedom, became an issue for Jesus and continued to be so for the apostles and the early church.

Jesus blasts the religious leaders, the scribes, and the

Pharisees in Matthew 23, pinpointing some enemies to the freedom found in the gospel. Jesus calls them hypocrites and outlines some of the issues He faced with them.

The Seat of Moses –

Jesus is not referring to a literal seat. Ironically, he uses the term "Moses seat" as an analogy to describe the throne of legalism and the root of all that became an enemy of the gospel of grace that Jesus and the apostles proclaimed.

"The scribes and the Pharisees sit in Moses' seat." Matthew 23:2.

It would appear that Jesus, in His discourse in Matthew 23, describes and rebukes these religious leaders who are supposed to be custodians of the law. Let me list a few things that Jesus highlights.

(a) **They were Hypocrites** – they say one thing but do another.

(b) **They lay heavy burdens on people** – They are not prepared to carry themselves or are willing to help relieve the burdens from others.

(c) **They like to be noticed by others** – By wanting the best seats in the synagogue.

(d) **They like to lord it over people** – By being spiritually superior to others.

(e) **They shut the door to the kingdom of God –**

By stopping others from entering because they opposed the gospel.

(f) **They Major in the little things and ignore what is important.**

(g) **They were like the blind leading the blind.**

Legalism and religion today –

There are things we are not to do, but that should not always be what we focus on. If we do, we are in danger of becoming legalistic and religious.

Unfortunately, legalism is still around in some churches where you feel under pressure to obey all the rules and conform to certain conditions to be a good Christian. These are often subtle and hard to discern. There are many traditional practices.

For example, some Christians today will only eat fish on Good Friday and abstain from consuming meat. It is out of respect for Christ, who died on the cross that day, but I have never fully understood why we have this tradition. Others get very fastidious with foods and dietary programs that may benefit our health, but let's not make them another legalistic ritual.

We had some lovely Christians who were tea totalers stay with us. They were horrified to find Rum and Raisin ice cream in our freezer. Not that we had a taste for rum; we just liked the ice cream. What would they have thought had they found our red wine and garlic mix? We can become so preoccupied by self-righteous rules that there is no room for grace. I Like the way Matt Chandler puts it-

"Without a heart transformed by the grace of Christ, we just continue to manage external and internal darkness." –Matt Chandler.

The god of this world system –

Let us not forget that satanic forces want to keep people in bondage. They oppose the freedom that the gospel of grace offers.

"But if our gospel is veiled, it is veiled to those who are perishing, whose minds the god of this age has blinded, who do not believe, lest the light of the glory of Christ, who is the image of God should shine on them." 2 Corinthians 4:3-4.

There is nothing Satan would like better than to keep people blind to the gospel of grace. He would rather see people perish and end up in hell rather than be saved and end up in heaven. But Christ has come to open the eyes of the blind to the gospel of grace and to free the captives.

BUT FOR THE GRACE OF GOD GO I

Chapter 12

Grace in the Book of Acts

The book of Acts is the unfolding story of the SPREAD of the gospel of grace like wildfire from the time of the resurrection and ascension of Jesus in Jerusalem to Samaria, Syria, Greece, Rome, and beyond.

It records the day of Pentecost, the growth and development of the early church, and the apostle's missionary journeys ending with Paul in Rome.

In his article on *"The Gospel in Acts,"* Justin S. Holcomb describes it this way, "The gospel spreads despite barriers of geography, ethnicity, culture, gender, and wealth."

In Acts, *"grace"* parallels *"the gospel."* Jesus' message is the *'word of His grace.'*

"I commend you to the 'word of His grace,' which is able to build you up and give you an inheritance among all those who are sanctified." Acts 20 32.

Notice how Paul says, *"the word of His grace"* can build you up and give you an inheritance. It is something the law could never do for us. The law was ready to condemn and judge us, but the gospel of grace forgives and frees us to obtain an eternal inheritance.

Grace in the early church

How did the Jews, having been instructed in all the rules concerning the keeping of the law for centuries, react when suddenly confronted with the gospel of grace? Most religious leaders opposed it, but there was a mixed reaction among the people.

"And with great power, the apostles gave witness to the resurrection of the Lord Jesus. And great grace was upon them all." Acts 4:33.

Yes, great grace was upon them all, including Jews, Gentiles, and especially the apostles. The Holy Spirit had been poured out upon the waiting disciples, enabling them to perform miracles testifying to the resurrection of Jesus. Grace was also extended to non-believers, encouraging them to turn to Christ.

"And through the hands of the apostles, many signs and wonders were done among the people."... *"Also a multitude gathered from the surrounding cities to Jerusalem, bringing sick people and those who were tormented by unclean spirits, and they were all healed."* Acts 5:12 & 16.

These miracles were taking place among all the people.

"And certain men came down from Judea and taught the brethren Unless you are circumcised according to the custom of Moses, you cannot be saved. Therefore when Paul and Barnabas had no small dissention and dispute with them, they determined that Paul and Barnabas and certain others of them should go up to Jerusalem, to the apostles and elders about this question." Acts 15:1-2.

When they discussed the matter at Jerusalem, Peter stood up and declared that God made no distinction between the Gentiles and the Jews.

Peter said, *"Now therefore, why do you test God by putting a yoke on the neck of the disciples, which neither our fathers or we were able to bear? But we believe that through the grace of the Lord Jesus Christ, we shall be saved in the same manner as they."* Acts 15:10-11.

Then, they all kept silent while Paul and Barnabas declared how many miracles and wonders God had worked through them among the Gentiles.

James had the final say in this matter. He confirmed what Peter had said, that there was no distinction between Jews and Gentiles regarding salvation through Christ and that the gospel was for all humanity.

James then summed up the situation by saying, *"Therefore I judge that we should not trouble those from among the Gentiles who are turning to God. But that we write to them to abstain from things polluted by idols, from sexual immorality, from things strangled, and from blood. For Moses has had throughout many generations those who preach him in every city, being read in the synagogues every Sabbath."* Acts 15:19-21.

They were all satisfied with this decision.

The Ministry of Apollos in Acts

Apollos was a Jew, born in Alexandria, Egypt, to Jewish parents. He knew the way of the Lord, and he had an understanding of the doctrine of Christ and had made a commitment but only knew of the baptism of John.

He was a brilliant speaker, ministering at Ephesus, and when Aquila and Priscilla heard him speak in the synagogue, they took him aside and expounded to him the way of the Lord more perfectly. He must have had a revelation of the grace of God.

"He greatly helped those who believed through grace, for he vigorously refuted the Jews publicly, showing from the scriptures that Jesus is the Christ." Acts 18:27-28.

He convinced believers they were saved by grace, not by keeping the law.

Testifying to the gospel of Grace

Paul shows us how he wants to end his life and ministry. God had called him to 'testify to the gospel of grace,' and he realises he may not have much time left and wants to finish his life continuing to do so.

"Nor do I count my life dear to myself, so that I may finish my race with joy, and the ministry which I received from the Lord Jesus to testify to the gospel of the grace of God. And indeed, now I know that you all, among whom I have gone preaching the gospel of the kingdom of God, will see my face no more." Acts 20:24-25.

He knows how important it is for believers to have a revelation of the grace of God and realise that they are not justified by the law but by faith in Christ.

We conclude that the biggest obstacle for believers to the grace of God in the early church was the pressures the Jews put on believers to revert to sections of the law.

Subtle differences today

We may not have pressure from the Jews in our Western World to conform to the law. But we have more subtle differences that undermine grace by certain doctrines and church rules that can border on legalism.

We also have more subtle things. When I began ministry, the leaders sat on the platform; then, it became the front row; now, in some churches, the leaders are required to sit among the congregation.

In some churches, I have noticed that offerings and communion are distributed from the back row (for the last shall be first). There is almost a false sense of humility in some of these practices. These are minor and make no difference, but they show us how easy it is to develop insignificant habits. Others have specific rules in their rituals and ceremonies for people to observe to be better Christians that supposedly impress God.

We need order, for God is not the author of confusion and chaos. ***"Let all things be done decently and in order."*** 1 Corinthians 14:40.

We may be inclined to change the order of things for the sake of change. But in doing so, let us avoid making any new religious rut and make room for God's grace and the Holy Spirit's spontaneity in our actions.

Chapter 13

Grace and the work of the Holy Spirit

Grace and the work of the Holy Spirit within us is an ongoing process. It is a work of transformation that changes us to be more like Christ and enables us to do whatever He has called us to do in life.

"Grace is the power of the Holy Spirit coming to us free of charge to enable you to do with ease what you could never do on your own with any amount of struggle and effort." –Joyce Meyer.

The Holy Spirit is God within us. Jesus said, "For without Me, you can do nothing." John 15:5. In the context of this scripture, God is constantly pruning us like a gardener so He can work in us the characteristics of the fruit of the Spirit. God is just as concerned with our character development as with our Charisma.

"But the fruit of the Spirit is love, joy, peace, patience,

kindness, goodness, faithfulness, gentleness, self-control. Against such, there is no law. Galatians 5:22-23. Walking in the Spirit is the grace of God and the Holy Spirit working together within us, enabling us to fulfill His purpose.

I wrote down this fitting definition recently but cannot remember where I read it or who wrote it, but it is appropriate for this chapter -

"Grace is an undeserved, unmerited gift from God that enables the power of the Holy Spirit to accomplish in and through you what you cannot do on your own." –Author unknown to me.

Noah found grace

The world was so wicked in the days of Noah; the Lord was sorry that he had made man. He was grieved in His heart and decided to destroy this evilness and start again.

"But Noah found grace in the eyes of the Lord. Noah was a just man, perfect in his generation; Noah walked with God." Genesis 6:8-9.

Noah found grace in the eyes of the Lord. How do we find grace today? You may be thinking that you do not measure up like Noah. That you have done things you are ashamed of and that you will never find grace in the eyes of the Lord.

Under the new covenant, you CAN find grace in the eyes of the Lord because He looks at you through the blood of Christ, who has atoned for your sins. It includes you and everyone today.

The Holy Spirit and Mary

Mary found favour (grace) and was chosen by God to conceive and give birth to Jesus, the Messiah.

"Then the angel said to her, "Do not be afraid, Mary, for you have found favour (grace) with the Lord. And behold you will conceive in your womb and bring forth a Son, and you shall call His name Jesus." Luke 1:30-31.

Mary asked the obvious question, seeing she was still a virgin. *"How can this be?"*

"How can this be, seeing I do not know a man?" And the angel answered and said to her, "The Holy Spirit will come upon you, and the power of the highest will overshadow you; therefore also the Holy One who is to be born will be called the Son of God." Luke 1:34-35.

We may not fully understand this process, but the Holy Spirit's miraculous work in Mary enabled her to conceive.

The Holy Spirit also works in us miraculously to enable us to be born again and become a child of God.

A radical change

When God steps into our life, a radical change takes place. Imagine what Mary had to go through as a young unmarried woman who became pregnant. She would have lost her reputation and faced ridicule by friends and family. It would have severely disrupted her lifestyle.

I know when I became a Christian, I was ridiculed by friends and family and, to some extent, lost my reputation and credibility. My close friends thought I had gone mad and had become a religious freak.

God seems more concerned for our eternal well-being than our immediate reputation. It may be in our best interest to lose our reputation if it means letting God have His way in our lives.

Jesus *"Made Himself of no reputation, taking the form of a bondservant, and coming in the likeness of men."* Philippians 2:7.

So when God steps into our lives through the Holy Spirit, it may mean a radical and disruptive change. It may mean a loss of reputation. It may not be easy initially, but it will be beneficial in the long run.

The process should be effortless

Although we may go through difficulties and struggles when we come to faith, the actual change or transformation in our lives should be relatively effortless; it is the work of the Holy Spirit within us. It differs from the law, where we must keep trying hard to keep all the rules. It takes a great deal of effort, all to no avail.

But we are no longer in bondage to the law; we have been set free and are now sons and daughters of God and joint heirs with Christ.

"God has sent forth the Spirit of His Son into our

hearts, crying out, "Abba Father." "Therefore you are no longer a slave but a son, and if a son, then an heir of God through Christ." Galatians 4:6-7.

If you are an heir, you do not have to strive to be a son or daughter of God; you already are righteous, lovable, and acceptable in the sight of God, thanks to His grace and your faith in Christ.

This transformation is from the inside out -

The Holy Spirit can transform our lives and bring change from the inside out. We can easily fall into the trap of working from the outside by trying to change ourselves by striving to perfect the flesh. It is the trap the Galatians had fallen into, trying to perfect themselves by adhering to parts of the law and becoming better Christians by working on the flesh. It is the Spirit in us that frees us.

"Now the Lord is the Spirit; and where the Spirit of the Lord is, there is liberty. But we all with unveiled face, beholding as in a mirror the glory of the Lord, are being transformed into the same image from glory to glory, just as by the Spirit of the Lord." 2 Corinthians 3:17-18.

The work of the Holy Spirit within is liberating; it transforms our life into the image of Christ. It is an ongoing work of grace from the inside out. It is not us trying to improve ourselves from the outside in. It should be effortless.

Transformation is not something we can accomplish on our own. We need the help of the Holy Spirit.

When Jesus was preparing the disciples for the future, He told them that He was going away but that they would never be left alone.

"I will pray the Father, and He will give you another Helper, that He may abide with you forever – the Spirit of truth, whom the world cannot receive because it neither sees Him nor knows Him; but you know Him, for He dwells WITH you and shall be IN you. I will not leave you as orphans; I will come to you." John 14:16-18.

Jesus refers to the Holy Spirit, who He said will be WITH and IN you. So, as Christians, we will never be abandoned and left alone like orphans.

The Holy Spirit is with and in us and doing continual work.

Let your light shine

Jesus encouraged His followers to let their light shine. He knew others would see something different about us.

"You are the light of the world." …. *"Let your light shine before men."* Matthew 5:14-16.

Paul implies the only hope of some people knowing Christ is because of Christ in you. They will notice something different about you because of who you are in Christ, not just what you do.

We found it very noticeable while we were in PNG that Christians had a radiance that seemed to lighten up their faces compared to non-Christians' who had a heaviness.

"Christ in you the hope of glory." Colossians 1:27.

You may be the only hope someone has of seeing something of God's glory because of God's grace and the work of the Holy Spirit within you.

The inner man

Jesus focused on the inner man when He forgave and healed the disabled man let down through the roof for Jesus to heal.

"When He saw their faith, He said to him, "Man, your sins are forgiven you." Luke 5:20.

What an anti-climax this must have been for those who had faith in a miracle and had gone through all that trouble of carrying the man and breaking into the roof to let him down so Jesus would heal him. All Jesus did was say, *"Your sins are forgiven you."* You can imagine their disappointment. They thought they were going to see him instantly healed.

Why did Jesus tell the man, *"Your sins are forgiven you?"* Why did he not just heal him and be done with it? I think it was twofold.

Firstly, for the man's sake. We do not know the background of this man. Maybe he needed to hear he was forgiven before being healed. Was the Holy Spirit at work within this man, performing an inner work of grace and healing?

Knowing that God forgives your sins and has removed the condemnation from your past is something we all need to hear.

Secondly, for the Scribes' and Pharisees' sake. When they heard Jesus say, *"Your sins are forgiven you,"* they were critical of Jesus, saying, *"Who can forgive sins but God alone?"* Verse 21. Jesus answers them with a question, *"Which is easier to say," " Your sins are forgiven you, or to say," "Rise up and walk?"* Verse 23.

Then to prove His point and show how easy it was for Him to forgive and heal the man, He said to them, *"But that you may know that the Son of Man has power on earth to forgive sins"* – He said to the man who was paralysed, *"I say to you, arise, take up your bed, and go to your house." Immediately he rose up before them and took up what he had been lying on, and departed to his own house, glorifying God.* Verse 24-25.

By doing this, He demonstrated that He was God, the Messiah, and all things were possible.

Nothing can hold you back

Things that condemn you from the past, fleshly sins, your failure to keep the law, and all the associated rules can never hold you back. They are now nailed to the cross.

"He made us alive together with Him, having forgiven you all trespasses, having wiped out the handwriting of requirements that was against us, which was contrary to us. And He has taken it out of the way, having nailed it to the cross. Having disarmed principalities and powers, He made a public spectacle of them, triumphing over them in it." Colossians 2:13-15

How good is that! It is in your face to our demonic enemies. It is a knockout blow. The things the devil would use to condemn us have been nailed to the cross, enabling us to walk in grace and victory over our enemies who judge us and make us feel guilty.

The law did not change people and never will. Grace enables us to change as we put our faith in Christ. The work of the Holy Spirit transforms us and changes us because of Christ within. So, we can be confident that God has not given up on us and is continually at work within us.

"Being confident of this very thing that He who begun a good work in you will complete it until the day of Jesus Christ." Philippians 1:6.

This transformation is an ongoing process; it is the grace of God and the work of the Holy Spirit within us. If Christianity is hard work for you, maybe you need to do less trying and be more trusting.

But for the GRACE of God go I

BUT FOR THE GRACE OF GOD GO I

Chapter 14

The Throne of Grace not judgment

The Throne of Grace is not to be confused with *"The Great White Throne,"* which speaks of the final judgment of humanity according to our works. Those not found in the Book of Life end up in the lake of fire with Satan and his fallen angels. (Revelation 21:11-13).

Jesus describes the Lake of Fire as a place of eternal torment and implies that we should avoid it at all costs. We can dodge the Lake of Fire by having our names written in the Book of Life. It will happen the moment you receive Christ as your Saviour and Lord. When the disciples were excited because demons were subject to them in Jesus' name, Jesus said, *"Rather, rejoice for your names are written in heaven."* Luke 10:20. He would have been referring to the Book of Life.

Is your name written in the Book of Life? If not, commit your life to Christ now, and it will be. I have heard some people say, *"But I would like to be with my mates in hell."* What a deception; if you end up in hell, you will curse your mates for being the reason you are there with them. Resist that temptation and receive Christ as your Lord and Saviour.

Most of us have probably seen works of art portraying **"The Great White Throne Judgment."** God usually sits on His throne, looking angry as he administers judgment.

Some images are graphic, portraying a fearsome-looking God who appears to show no mercy or grace. Yes, there will be a time of judgment. But some of these works of art conjure up the wrong image of God regarding the "throne of grace" that is now available to us.

The Throne of God in Heaven

Before we examine the throne of grace, let us pause and consider some fantastic descriptions of the throne of God in Heaven.

There are majestic scenes that are so incredible you would find it hard to believe that God would ever be approachable.

Let us look at some scriptures that glimpse some of these incredible sights focused around the throne of God set in Heaven.

"There was the likeness of a throne, in appearance like a sapphire stone; on the likeness of a throne was a likeness of the appearance of a man high above it. Also, from the appearance of His waist and upward, I saw

as it were the colour of amber with the appearance of fire all around within it; and from the appearance of His waist and downward, I saw, as it were, he appearance of fire with brightness all around. Like the appearance of a rainbow in a cloud on a rainy day, so was the appearance of brightness all around it."

This was the appearance of the likeness of the glory of the Lord. Ezekiel 1:26-28.

"I watched till thrones were put in place, and the Ancient of Days was seated; His garment was white as snow, and the hair of His head was like pure wool. His throne was a fiery flame, its wheels a burning fire." Daniel 7:9.

In writing to Timothy, Paul describes the Lord in His immortal, eternal state as so awesome that He dwells in unapproachable light.

"The only Potentate, the King of kings and Lord of lords, who alone has immortality, dwelling in unapproachable light, whom no man has seen or can see, to whom be honour and everlasting power. Amen." 1 Timothy 6:15-16.

In the book of Revelation, John gives us a picture of the Lord in His eternal glory, which is so awesome that he was startled by His appearance.

"One like the Son of Man clothed with a garment down to the feet and girded about the chest with a golden

band. *His head and hair were white like wool, as white as snow, and His eyes like a flame of fire; His feet were like brass as if refined in a furnace, and His voice as the sound of many waters. He had in His right hand seven stars, and out of His mouth went a sharp two-edged sword, and His countenance like the sun shining in its strength."* Revelation 1:13-16.

Paul says He *"dwells in unapproachable light."* John says in Revelation, *"like the sun shining in its strength,"* if you could approach the sun, you would not get far; you would disintegrate from the intense heat. How approachable was the Lord in this form?

When John saw Him in this form, he said, *"I fell at His feet as dead."* Then we read, *"He laid His right hand on me, saying to me, "Do not be afraid; I am the First and the Last." "I am He who lives and was dead, and behold, I am alive forever more. Amen. And I have the keys of Hades and of Death."* Revelation 1:17-18.

How wonderful! The Lord lays His hand on John and tells him not to be afraid, assuring him that He is the same Jesus John was with on earth, and He is now victorious and invincible and holds the keys of hell and death.

The Throne of Grace today

A throne of grace seems contradictory to some scenes we have been looking at, but Christians are encouraged to come to the *"throne of grace"* today in this dispensation of grace. Not to a throne of Judgment.

"Seeing then we have a great High Priest who has passed through the heavens, Jesus the Son of God, let us hold fast our confession. For we do not have a High Priest who cannot sympathise with our weaknesses but was in all points tempted as we are, yet without sin. Let us, therefore, come boldly to the throne of grace, that we may obtain mercy and find grace to help in time of need." Hebrews 4:14-16.

Some things we need to understand about the Throne of Grace -

1. Jesus is our High Priest in Heaven

We are coming to Jesus, our High Preist, who can identify with all our weaknesses. He was tempted in all points, just as we are today, yet He was without sin.

2. We are to hold fast to our confession

We are justified through faith in Christ and not our self-righteous works. No matter what condemnation man or the devil may unload on us, our faith in Christ justifies us.

3. We are to come boldly

The word boldly comes from the Greek word *"Parrhesia,"* which, when used in ancient times, referred to freedom of speech. We should not hold back but be upfront, bold, and honest before the Lord.

4. We will obtain mercy and grace

We are looking for this to help us in our time of need. Whatever that need may look like, mercy and grace will help us get through it so we can resume a life of victory.

God wants us to come to Him boldly, unlike a fearful dog whimpering with its tail between its legs.

How is this possible?

Why do we now have a throne of grace, not judgment? What made the difference? How is this currently possible?

The answer is simple.

The throne of grace is a bit like the *"mercy seat"* on the ark of the covenant in the Tabernacle, where the high priest would sprinkle the blood of animals to atone for the people's sins. God would look at the blood and NOT judge the people according to the law inside the ark they had broken. It is why we obtain mercy when we come to the throne of grace.

When we look at the throne in the book of Revelation, we see the Lamb (Jesus), who was slain on earth, is on the throne, now making it possible for us to come boldly through His shed blood.

"Worthy is the Lamb who was slain. To receive power riches and wisdom, and strength and honour and glory and blessing...Be to Him who sits on the throne, and to the Lamb, for ever and ever." Revelation 5:11-13.

How often should we come to the throne of grace? As much as we like, whenever we want to. There is never a time when it is inappropriate. He is always available. He is now approachable, so let us take advantage of this invitation and come boldly.

I would shut the door while preparing my Sunday sermon, and I became unapproachable until one of my children was sobbing at the door and needed their daddy. I was about to say go away, come back later, but the Holy Spirit convicted me and said, *"Jesus never shut the door on anyone."* So I opened the door and gave them a much-needed hug. I still valued my privacy, but the door was always open to them.

Abundant grace to reign in life

When we link the throne of grace to Romans chapter 5, we have the key to reigning in life here and now before we get to heaven.

"For if by one man's offense death reigned through the one, much more those who receive abundance of grace and of the gift of righteousness will reign in life through the one Jesus Christ." Romans 5:17.

Sin, death, judgment, and condemnation that came through one man, Adam, no longer controls our lives. We have now received abundant grace and the gift of righteousness through one man, Christ. Applying this abundance of grace to our lives will enable us to reign in life.

It is not something we have to earn or work for; it is to be received and applied to our lives in faith. It will liberate you to live in victory.

Jesus came to save, not judge

Jesus did not come to judge and condemn the world; He came to save the world.

"For God did not send His Son into the world to condemn the world, but that the world through Him might be saved." John 3:17.

So, do not hesitate to come boldly to the throne of grace, having confidence that you are coming to obtain mercy and grace from a loving God.

Chapter 15

Shouts of Grace Grace

Grace Grace, No, it's not a spelling mistake.

It is not about shouting accolades to the name of a Queensland politician who goes by the name of "Grace Grace." Her maiden name is "Ingazia Graziella Farfiglia." "Graziella" in Italian means "Grace." She then married Michael Grace, hence the name "Grace Grace."

"Shouts of Grace Grace" is an exciting phrase used in scripture that we will unpack.

"This is the word of the Lord to Zerubbabel: Not by might nor by power but by My Spirit, Says the Lord of Hosts. Who are you, O great mountain? Before Zerubbabel, you shall become a plain! And he shall bring forth the capstone With shouts of grace, grace to it." Zechariah 4:6-7.

He shall bring forth the capstone with shouts of Grace

Grace, which is a key to understanding an important aspect of grace. We will come back to this, but let us look at the context of this scripture first.

Who was Zerubbabel?

The word of the Lord came to Zerubbabel. Who was Zerubbabel? He had originally been in Babylon, a Jew who returned to Jerusalem at the head of a band of Jewish exiles and became governor of Judea under the Persians. Influenced by the prophets Haggai and Zechariah, he was rebuilding the Temple.

"Then the prophet Haggai and Zechariah the son of Iddo, prophets prophecied to the Jews who were in Judea and Jerusalem, in the name of the God of Israel, who was over them. So Zerubbabel the son of Shealtiel and Jeshua the son of Jozadak rose up and began to build the house of God which is in Jerusalem; and the prophets of God were with them, helping them." Ezra 5:1-2.

Zerubbabel had laid the foundation for the Temple. However, the rebuilding of the Temple had stalled as there was continual opposition.

"The hands of Zerubbabel have laid the foundation of this Temple; His hands shall also finish it. Then you shall know that the Lord of Hosts has sent Me to you. For who has despised the day of small things." Zechariah 4:9-10.

I am sure we have all faced opposition if we have tried to

build a church in any way, shape, or form.

Years ago, we were trying to plant a church in Healesville, not far from Melbourne. We would drive from Melbourne to hold meetings every weekend. We had been going for a few months and had opposition. Louts threw stones on the roof of where we held the meetings, and only a few people had turned up.

After a hard weekend, I was about to give up. I knelt and prayed, *"Lord, I think I should quit."* Then, looking for an answer, I opened my bible at random (not a recommended practice) and read, ***"But the end is not yet."*** (Matthew 24:6). I thought that was a fluke, then I opened it again and read, ***"Do not despise small beginnings."*** (the above scripture). So we battled on, and by the grace of God, at the end of twelve months, we had a great group of about forty people. It ended up being a successful church plant as I handed it over to another pastor and accepted the invitation to join the team of a thriving Charismatic church in Melbourne.

God gave Zerubbabel a promise that He would take care of the opposition. He was facing a mountain of problems created by his enemies.

"Who are you, O great mountain? Before Zerubbabel, you shall become a plain!" Verse 7a.

God promises those mountains of opposition will become a plain before Zerubbabel. But he still has to do something for this to happen, which is the key to this story.

Take the capstone

He had to take the capstone. It was crucial because the capstone signified that the building was complete. It was the last piece of the construction put in place. It was the finishing stone of the structure, the crowning achievement.

So God asked Zerubbabel to uphold a vision to complete the Temple. He was to stop looking at the mountain of opposition and the unfinished Temple and start seeing the finished Temple by faith.

Shout "Grace Grace" to it

As Zerubbabel visualised the capstone on the building, he was to shout *"Grace Grace"* to it. He was to do this continually while they were building it. In other words, by the grace of God, this will be completed despite the opposition. It was a bold shout of *"Grace Grace,"* not a whisper.

Jentezen Franklin tells the story of when they were building their church auditorium, they had lots of opposition. But every time he drove past the construction site, he would wind the window down, point, and shout *"Grace Grace"* to it. When he had the family on board, they would all join in. They did this by faith until the building was complete.

How is this possible?

By grace, the Holy Spirit is at work on our behalf. It is not just our administration and self-effort that gets the job done; it is not our power or might; it is the power and might of the Holy

Spirit that enables us to finish what we started.

"Not by might nor by power, but by my Spirit, says the Lord of Hosts." Verse 6.

The late Trevor Chandler used this verse as the motto for his church and ministry for many years. Trevor was very successful as a pastor and evangelist, seeing many people come to Christ.

Maybe you are facing a mountain of opposition. It may be spiritual, physical, or financial, and something has stalled and is unfinished.

Then, start visualising how you want it to look when it is finished, and shout *"Grace Grace"* to it by faith in Jesus' Name until it is complete.

BUT FOR THE GRACE OF GOD GO I

Chapter 16

A Safety Net of Grace

We hear of people who have fallen from grace. It is an idiom referring to those who lose their position of power, respect, credibility, status, and prestige.

It can apply to anybody. We usually hear of those in the public eye who fall from grace. They could be in leadership positions in government, in business, in the movies, or even in the church.

We want to look at this from a Christian perspective. Is it possible to fall from grace? Can Christians lose their salvation? Do we have a safety net of grace if we fall away from God? Or are we like some trapeze artists who perform without a safety net?

The short answer is no, we are not without a safety net, but can we justify this from scripture?

"The steps of a good man are ordered by the Lord,

and He delights in his way. Though he fall, he shall not be utterly cast down; For the Lord upholds him with His hand." Psalm 37:23-24.

After reading the above scripture, we could almost stop and say, *"Case closed."* If the good man falls, he is not down and out. He is still in the race. The Lord upholds him. The hand of the Lord is his safety net.

"For a righteous man may fall seven times and rise again, but the wicked shall fall by calamity" Proverbs 24:16.

The implication is that the righteous man has a safety net, a bit like a trampoline, and though he falls, he will rise again. As Christians, we should be encouraged by these scriptures. I would encourage you not to wallow in self-pity. Do not let the devil put his foot on your neck and try and hold you down. Get up, and by the grace of God, bounce back again.

We have other scriptures that refer to falling from grace. But we need to look at the context.

"You have become estranged from Christ, you who attempt to be justified by the law; you have fallen from grace." Galatians 5:4.

The above verse does not necessarily refer to falling away from God. It relates to someone who has fallen back to relying on the law for their justification. So they have fallen from grace by doing so; instead of being justified through faith in Jesus Christ, they are now trying to keep the law to justify their relationship with God.

There must be a safety net of grace for such a person. Once they come to their senses and realise how futile it is to try and justify themselves by trying to keep the law, they will have the opportunity to fall back on the grace of God and faith in Christ for their justification.

A debatable scripture

Here is a difficult scripture to interpret.

"For it is impossible for those who were once enlightened, and have tasted the heavenly gift, and have become partakers of the Holy Spirit, and have tasted the good word of God and the powers of the age to come, if they fall away, to renew them again to repentance, since they crucify again for themselves the Son of God, and put Him to an open shame." Hebrews 6:4-6.

Does this indicate that God takes away the safety net of grace for these people?

It looks that way, but we must ask several questions about these verses. Who are these people? We are not sure who they are or how they were once enlightened; they had heard and knew the gospel, but had they been born again, or was it head knowledge? How committed were they in the first place? How had they tasted the heavenly gift? How did they partake of the Holy Spirit? And to what extent did they fall away?

Some Scholars say they were probably those who were

exposed to the gospel, having an intellectual understanding of it, but were never really born again. They could have been people who knew the truth but were not fully committed to following Christ.

The worst-case scenario would be that they were Christians who had come so far, then, for some unexplainable reason, turned their back on Christ, denied Him, approved of His crucifixion, and took a stand against Christ. They chose to become anti-Christian and were beyond redemption.

But once again, if they were genuine and had received the gift of salvation. It is a gift and not a loan, which would indicate that there was still a safety net in place if they needed it, but maybe by their own free will, they did not want it because they had no intention of becoming committed Christians.

A friend who had fallen away

When we were holidaying in Melbourne some time ago, my wife and her sister Jill wanted to catch up with an old girlfriend. They had attended the same church as teenagers; she had been a dedicated Christian. We arranged to meet her and her husband for coffee. During the conversation, my wife asked her what church she was going to these days.

Her reply stunned us. We were in a state of shock. She said, *"I don't go to church anymore. I have become an atheist. I no longer believe in God."* Fishing for an answer, I asked her, *"Why did you decide to do that?"* She said, *"I don't know, it just happened."*

I felt her answer was hiding something, and there was much

more to it, but I did not pursue it. We came away in disbelief. How could it just happen?

The obvious question is, does she still have a safety net of grace to fall back on? It is hard to say, but I would like to think so. Should she realise that she has made a terrible decision and wants to turn back to Christ like the prodigal son, she would hopefully have a safety net of grace.

Did Satan fall from grace?

Jesus said He saw Satan fall from heaven.

"I saw Satan fall like lightning from heaven" Luke 10:18. In the following scripture, we see how and why this happened.

"How are you fallen from heaven, O Lucifer, son of the morning! How are you cut down to the ground, you who weakened the nations? For you have said in your heart: I will ascend into heaven, I will exalt my throne above the stars of God; I will also sit on the mount of the congregation On the farthest sides of the north; I will ascend above the heights of the clouds, I will be like the Most High. Yet you shall be brought down to Sheol, to the lowest depths of the pit." Isaiah 14:12-15.

Satan did not fall from grace. He was cast down because of His pride and rebellion against God.

The five *"I wills"* in the above verses reveal his pride and rebellion.

1. I will ascend into heaven.
2. I will exalt my throne above the stars of God.
3. I will sit on the mount of the congregation.
4. I will ascend above the heights.
5. I will be like the Most High.

"God resists the proud but gives grace to the humble." James 4:6. There is no humility with Satan, only pride and rebellion against God. He will never humble himself.

We read more about the fall of Satan in the Book of Revelation.

"And war broke out in heaven: Michael and his angels fought with the dragon, and the dragon and his angels fought, but they did not prevail, nor was there a place found for them in heaven any longer. So the great dragon was cast out, that serpent of old called the Devil and Satan, who deceives the whole world; he was cast to the earth, and his angels were cast out with him." Revelation 12:7-9.

So, he did not fall from grace. There was no longer a place in heaven for him. He was cast out and will end up in a bottomless pit. Therefore, he will fall for a long time because he has no safety net. His fall will take him into the pit of hell, and he will be damned to spend eternity there.

The problem for us today is that Satan would like to deceive the whole world and cause as many people as possible to fall into hell with him.

David's fall from grace

David is a sober reminder of how easy it is to fall from grace. He was one of the heroes of faith. He faced Goliath, slew him, and did many other exploits in the name of the Lord.

Yet, David fell from grace by committing adultery with Bathsheba and then arranged to have her husband go to the front line of the battlefield. David plotted to get rid of him and hoped he would die in the heat of the fighting. David schemed all this to take Bathsheba as his wife.

The prophet Nathan had exposed his sin so David could no longer hide it. They were to learn that grace does not erase the consequences of their sin. The child born to them was to die. But there remained a safety net of grace for both David and Bathsheba.

"I have sinned against the Lord." And Nathan said to David. The Lord also has put away your sin; you shall not die. However, because by this deed you have given great occasion to the enemies of the Lord to blaspheme, the child also who is born to you shall surely die." 2 Chronicles 12: 13-14.

His acknowledgment of sin was the turning point for David to repent and seek restoration. He cried out to God to blot out this terrible transgression and sought the presence of the Lord.

"Have mercy on me, O God, according to your loving-kindness; according to the multitude of your tender mercies, blot out my transgressions. Wash me thoroughly from my iniquity, and cleanse me from my sin." "Do not cast me away from Your presence, and do not take Your Holy Spirit from me." Psalm 51: 1-2 & 11

David was eventually restored in his fellowship with God and continued to serve the Lord.

The church as a safety net

The church's track record in some areas has not been all that good. Yet, despite the church being mocked and ridiculed, it is a safety net that God has provided. The church is responsible for proclaiming the gospel to get people saved, bring Christians to maturity, and keep them following the Lord.

In his book *"What's So Amazing about Grace,"* Philip Yancey sums up his experience by saying -

"I rejected the church because I found so little grace there. I returned to the church because I found grace nowhere else."

Jesus raises the bar by saying, **"Therefore you shall be perfect, just as your Father in heaven is perfect."** Matthew 5:48.

Perfect can also mean being complete, whole, fully developed, and righteous. The only way is through His grace and atonement for our sins.

On the one hand, it seems Jesus is setting an unattainable

standard. On the other hand, He lowers the safety net of grace by offering forgiveness and salvation to the adulterous woman, the prostitute, the thief next to Him on the cross, His disciple Peter, who denied he ever knew Him, Saul (Paul), the apostle who had persecuted the church.

The church proclaiming a gospel of grace is a safety net for all who will believe.

BUT FOR THE GRACE OF GOD GO I

Chapter 17

Faith in Future Grace

The past is gone, and you can do nothing about it.

Not even God can change the past. From the moment you read this, the rest of your life will be in the future.

One of the verses to the Hymn *"Amazing Grace"* sums up what I am trying to convey in this chapter –

"Through many dangers, toils, and snares,

I have already come;

'Tis grace that brought me safe thus far,

And grace will lead me home."

Regardless of what you have been through up until now, grace has enabled you to survive. Therefore, you can only expect grace to continue to revive you and lead you home to eternity.

A quote from D. L. Moody also expounds what I want to explain throughout this chapter. We never run out of grace, just as it was available in the past, so it will be available each day in the future as we need it.

"A man can no more take in a supply of grace for the future than he can eat enough today to last him for the next six months, nor can he inhale sufficient air into his lungs with one breath to sustain life for a week to come. We are permitted to draw upon God's store of grace from day to day as we need it." – Dwight L Moody.

We live in a volatile, unpredictable world. We do not know what is going to happen in the future.

Dr. Barry Chant wrote this poem inspired by terrible wars in 2023 that are continuing into 2024 and the world's desperate need for a Saviour.

The Gentleness of Grace

The soldiers crouched in trenches,
rockets swooshing overhead;
while drones slipped through defenses,
bullets left a trail of dead.
'My wife can't understand it,
why we risk our lives out here
and the generals sit back safely
free from danger, death, and fear.'
As the sergeant spoke, he grimaced,
'Has there ever been a Head
who would give himself to battle
while his troops go home instead?'

Yes, there has! His name is Jesus
And he turned it all around;
It was He who won the victory
and took back the stolen ground.
He came to earth in weakness
and the gentleness of grace;
so we reign with Him in glory
who is Lord of time and space!
– Barry Chant 2023.

We could look at the potential conflicts between many nations, worldwide environmental issues, and failing economies. Also, there are numerous biblical signs leading to the return of Christ. But I do not want to dwell on things that may affect the future. I desire to focus on the grace that will help us cope with whatever the future holds.

Be strong in Grace

Paul instructs young Timothy, who has his future life in front of him, to be strong in the grace that is in Christ Jesus.

"You, therefore, my son, be strong in the grace that is in Christ Jesus." …. *"You therefore must endure hardship as a good soldier of Jesus Christ."* 2 Timothy 2:1 & 3.

Paul tells Timothy to be strong in grace because of the hardships he will face. Paul does not promise Timothy that life will be a bed of roses; he tells him to endure hardship as a good soldier.

Paul knows too well that Timothy will have his battles and must be strong in grace.

Grace gives us the confidence to see our vision and dreams fulfilled. It empowers us to believe that God will honour His promises in the future because of His grace toward us now and in the past.

It is not an unattainable grace, a way off in the future somewhere. It is not some pie in the sky that we have to keep striving for.

It is having confidence that His grace will be there for us when we need it most in the future.

Grace is not like the cat who supposedly only has nine lives. It is not something we use up and run out of. God does not say, "Bad luck, you have run out of grace; you have used up your quota!" His grace will always sustain us now and into the future.

Your future hopes rest upon grace

Whatever hopes you have for the future, rest them upon Grace. Whatever plans you have, be confident you can achieve them because of His grace.

"...rest your hope fully upon the grace that is to be brought to you at the revelation (appearing) of Jesus Christ; as obedient children, not conforming yourselves to the former lusts, as in your ignorance; but as He who has called you is holy, you also be holy, in all your

conduct, because it is written, "Be holy for I am holy." 1 Peter 1:13-16.

Our conduct should be holy (sanctified) and pleasing to God. However, we realise that this is only possible because of the grace of God.

The same grace that led us to turn to Christ for salvation will continue to be with us until we enter eternity. We can never earn our salvation. It is the gift of God. Therefore, rest your future hopes and dreams upon His grace.

No matter your past, grace will allow you to reach your full potential in God.

Before his encounter with Christ, the apostle Paul was a zealous Jew persecuting Christians and the Church. However, by the grace of God, he was saved and eventually became an apostle. He says he is not worthy to be called an apostle but is what he is by the grace of God.

Grace was in the past; regarding his conversion, it was present working in him to cause him to labour to be an apostle, and it was continually with him for the rest of his life.

Paul begins and ends his letters

Paul deals with doctrinal issues of correction, discipline, and sanctification in the church. However, noting how he begins and ends his letters with a salutation of grace is interesting.

In most of Paul's letters, he begins with the phrase, **"Grace to you and peace from God our Father and the Lord Jesus**

Christ." (Galatians 1:3). It seems like he desires to introduce grace to the believers through his letters.

But, he closes most of his letters with the phrase, ***"The grace of the Lord Jesus Christ be with you all."*** (Philippians 4:23).

It carries with it the thought of the grace of God being with you as you go on your way into the future. Whatever that may hold for you, you can face it because the grace of God will be with you.

So we ask again, *"What is future grace?"* His grace carries us through life from one moment to the next, from one experience to the next, from one trial to the next, from one setback to the next, or one victory to the next.

No matter our state, His grace is sufficient for us. God can only count us worthy of His calling upon our lives because of His grace. Yes, His grace will empower us as we continue to follow Christ.

Should we try and pay God back?

In his book *"Future Grace"* John Piper has a section on whether we should try and pay God back out of gratitude for His Grace. He calls it the *"debtor's ethic."* Let me share with you an extract from this section in his book.

"The debtor's ethic says because you have done something good for me, I feel indebted to do something good for you. This impulse is not what gratitude was meant to produce. God meant gratitude to be a spontaneous expression of pleasure in the gift and goodwill of another. He did not mean

it to be an impulse to return favours. If gratitude is twisted into a sense of debt, it gives birth to the debtor's ethic - the effect is to nullify grace."

He is not saying we should not express gratitude as God expects it. He is implying that gratitude is vulnerable. Many believe they should pay God back and serve Him out of gratitude for His grace.

We have instances in the bible, and we have all heard of others, and perhaps we have ourselves made vows to God. They are debtors' payback vows, *"God if you do this, I will do that."* Although God may have honoured these vows, it misses the point of free grace; it is no longer free but servile. The grace of God was given to you for salvation as you put your faith in Christ. This grace has never been withdrawn and never will be. It is with you into the future and will be there for you when you need it most.

You can not earn grace. You are thankful for it, and out of gratitude, you can give God thanks for it. But it is a gift, and you are not in debt to somehow have to pay God back for it.

BUT FOR THE GRACE OF GOD GO I

Chapter 18

Portals of Grace

I will not focus on the word *"grace"* in this last chapter except for one crucial scripture. I believe what I share gives us insight and *"food for thought"* to an exciting concept that is possible by the grace of God.

What is a portal? A portal is a door that leads from one space or environment to another.

If you enter your house, you are stepping from an outside environment to an inside environment. Then, as you walk through your home from one door to the next, you are transitioning from the hallway to the lounge, to the dining, to the kitchen, and so on. As you pass through each doorway, you enter a slightly different environment.

In the *'Chronicles of Nania,'* C. S. Lewis has four siblings going into a wardrobe used as a portal, and they enter into Nania Land, a make-believe world, for an incredible adventure.

J. R. R. Tolkien, whose book series *"Lord of the Rings"* still leaves fans hungering for a portal of their own to enter his Middle-earth. (which is like a substitute for the Garden of Eden or Heaven).

We also have testimonies and books written by people who have died, visited heaven, and returned. Most tell of entering a dark tunnel and moving toward a bright light, the Lord or Heaven. Could this be like a portal to another dimension?

I enjoy some science fiction movies and am always fascinated by portals like those in the Stargate series. You see a portal open, and someone steps through it and enters another world that could be light-years away from Earth.

Possible Portals in Scripture

I want to suggest the Bible indicates that there are possible portals of grace that open from Earth into heaven or the realm of the Spirit. I will explain by looking at several examples in scripture.

Jacobs Ladder –

"Then he dreamed, and behold, a ladder was set up on the earth, and its top reached to heaven; and there the angels of God were ascending and descending on it" Genesis 28:12.

Did Jacob dream of one of these portals between earth and heaven? In this case, it is a portal that angels use.

Then Jacob awoke and said, *"Surely the Lord is in this*

place, and I did not know it." And he was afraid and said, "How awesome is this place! This is none other than the house of God, and this is the gate of heaven." Genesis 28:16-17.

It took place at Bethel, which means "House of God," implying that this could be the gate of heaven. Is this typifying the church?

Therefore, the church proclaiming the gospel could be another subtle gate, portal, or doorway to heaven.

Elijah and his chariot of fire –

"Then it happened, as they continued on and talked, that suddenly a chariot of fire appeared with horses of fire and separated the two of them; and Elijah went up by a whirlwind into heaven." 2 Kings 2:11.

Could this be a portal opening up to take Elijah into heaven? For Elijah not to experience death was undoubtedly God's grace in action.

Elijah's servant, Elisha, caught the mantle Elijah dropped when the chariot whisked him into heaven. Elijah had promised Elisha a double portion of the Spirit if he took the mantle.

After taking the mantle, Elisha Stuck the waters of the Jordan River and said,

"Where is the Lord God of Elijah?" Verse 14. The river parted this way and that, and Elisha crossed over. We have a

biblical record of Elisha performing twice as many miracles as Elijah.

Elisha and his servant see into another realm –

The King of Syria was at war with Israel and was mad at Elisha, who could tell the king of Israel what he was up to. So the king of Syria heard where Elisha was in Dothan and sent an army to surround him. When Elisha's servant rose early one morning and went outside, he saw this army surrounding the city with horses and chariots.

And his servant went back and said, *"Alas, my master! What shall we do? So he answered, "Do not fear, for those who are with us are more than those who are with them." And Elisha prayed, saying, "Lord, I pray open his eyes that he may see." Then the Lord opened the eyes of the young man, and he saw.*

"And behold the mountain was full of horses and chariots of fire all around Elisha." 2 Kings 6:15-17.

God opened a door or a portal so the servant could see into the realm of the spirit. Elisha had already seen what was happening.

To finish the story, Elisha prayed for the Lord to blind the surrounding army, and then he led them away to Samaria. Elisha asked the Lord if he could kill them. The Lord said no, put on a great feast for them, and feed them. So he did, and they went away and did not attack Israel again. It was God extending His grace to them.

Jesus on the mount of transfiguration –

"Jesus took Peter, James, and John his brother, led them up on a high mountain by themselves; and He was transfigured before them. His face shone like the sun, and His clothes became as white as light. And behold, Moses and Elijah appeared to them and talked with Him." Matthew 17:1-3.

For Moses and Elijah to appear with a transfigured Jesus, you would think that some portal was opened between Earth and Heaven, giving the disciples a glimpse of another dimension.

What an incredible experience for those disciples who were with Jesus. It would seem that this was indeed another act of grace.

The stoning of Stephen –

Stephen rebuked those trying to keep the law, and they became angry with him; as they were ready to stone him, a portal opened, enabling him to gaze up into Heaven.

"But he being full of the Holy Spirit, gazed into heaven and saw the glory of God, and Jesus standing at the right hand of God, and said, "Look! I see the heavens opened and the son of Man standing at the right hand of God!" Acts 7:55-56.

Stephen was about to die, but by the grace of God, he could glimpse what to expect and look forward to as he entered heaven and into the Glory of God.

The apostle Paul caught up to the third heaven –

"Such a one was caught up to the third heaven. And I know such a man – whether in the body or out of the body I do not know, God knows – how he was caught up into Paradise and heard inexpressible words, which is not lawful for a man to utter." 2 Corinthians 12:2-4.

Paul seems unclear as to what happened to him. But could this have been another portal between earth and heaven, that he was caught up in heaven and heard things he was not permitted to utter?

Whatever happened, you would have to conclude that it was an act of grace extended to Paul.

John and the book of revelation –

In the book of Revelation, we have multiple portals or doors opening up between Earth and Heaven.

For example, *"After these things I looked, and behold, a door standing open in heaven."* Revelation 4:1.

John describes some beautiful glimpses of heaven, centered mainly around the Throne of God. I will leave it to you to explore this incredible book.

A portal for you to use today

In my opening statement to this chapter, I said, *"I will not focus on the word "grace" except for one crucial scripture."*

This scripture assures us of a portal of grace to help us through life right here and now. The portal speaks of coming to the throne of grace in prayer.

"Let us therefore come boldly to the throne of grace, that we may obtain mercy and find grace to help in time of need." Hebrews 4:16.

It is a beautiful invitation to come boldly to a God who will not judge us but impart mercy and grace in our time of need.

I will not elaborate on this as I have already done so in chapter 14 - *"The Throne of Grace, not Judgment."* To refresh your memory, I suggest you go back to that chapter where I fully expound on how to use this portal and how it will help you live in victory and reign in life.

What about you?

Are you using this portal of prayer today? It can change your life and your relationship with God.

Are you ready for heaven? When you die, will a portal be opened for you? Will you be caught up to spend eternity in heaven? You may feel that you are not worthy, do not deserve it, and can do nothing to earn it. But by the grace of God, it can happen for you.

The Bible declares salvation is the gift of God. The best gift you can ever hope for is eternal life. It is yours by grace through faith in Christ.

If you are reading this and you would like to come to faith in Christ I invite you to say this prayer...

"Lord Jesus, I come to you now and ask for your forgiveness. Come into my life and make me a new person. I believe in my heart and confess with my mouth that you are now my Saviour and Lord."

"For by grace you have been saved through faith, and that not of yourselves; it is the gift of God, not of works lest anyone should boast." Ephesians 2:8-9.

Jesus himself is the door or portal for our entrance into heaven. He said, **"I am the door. If anyone enters by Me, he will be saved and will go in and out and find pasture."** John 10:9.

Thank you for reading this book. I hope it has helped you to understand the Amazing Grace of God.

I have been personally blessed in writing it, as it has stirred my heart again to appreciate and appropriate the grace of God. I hope it does the same for you. May the grace of God be with you!

www.ingramcontent.com/pod-product-compliance
Lightning Source LLC
Chambersburg PA
CBHW031250290426
44109CB00012B/521